# I, Daniel Blake

Written by Paul Laverty
Directed by Ken Loach
Produced by Rebecca O'Brien

route

First published in 2016 by Route
PO Box 167, Pontefract, WF8 4WW
info@route-online.com
www.route-online.com

In association with Sixteen Films
2nd Floor, 187 Wardour Street, London, W1F 8ZB

ISBN: 978-1-901927-67-2

Cover design:
GOLDEN
From artwork supplied by Entertainment One UK Ltd

A catalogue for this book is available from the British Library

Printed in EU by Pulsio SARL

# Contents

**Paul Laverty**
*Writer*

Rebecca (Producer) and I didn't think it would take Ken long before he wanted to sink his teeth into something fresh after *Jimmy's Hall*, despite the rumours. It didn't.

It was a rich cocktail that seeped into what became *I, Daniel Blake*.

The sustained and systematic campaign against anyone on welfare spearheaded by the right-wing press, backed by a whole wedge of poisonous TV programmes jumping on the same bandwagon, caught our eye. Much of it was crude propaganda, savouring the misery of often pathetic characters in the most prurient fashion. And all the better if they had a drink problem, a sure sign of them wasting precious tax payers' money.

Little wonder it led to a spectacular aberration. Studies found that the average person thought that in excess of 30% of welfare payments were claimed fraudulently. The truth is that it is 0.7%. It was no surprise to find out that many people on benefits had been insulted and humiliated, with a significant number being attacked physically.

This manipulated distortion dovetailed perfectly with the austerity narrative by the Government and welfare cuts became a prime target. Who can forget Osborne's speech on the 'closed curtains' of the hordes of skivers still asleep in the early morning at the last Tory party conference? Another fact: only 3% of welfare budget goes to the unemployed while the elderly – the Tory preferred constituency – takes 42% in pensions.

But the immediate spark for this story started with a call I got from Ken to join him on a visit to his childhood home of Nuneaton where he has close connection with a charity that deals with homelessness. We met some terrific workers and they introduced us to some of the youngsters they were working with. One lad whom they had recently helped, shared his life story with us. It was his casual mention of hunger and description of nausea and light headedness as he tried to work (as usual, zero-hour contracts with precarious work on an ad hoc basis) that really struck us.

As Ken and I travelled the country, one contact leading to another, we heard many stories. Foodbanks became a rich source of information. It struck us that when we made *My Name is Joe* or *Sweet Sixteen*, or even going further back to Ken's earlier films, one of the big differences now was the new world of foodbanks.

As more and more stories came to light, we realised that many people are now making a choice between food or heat. We met a remarkable man in Scotland, principled and articulate, desperate to work, who refused point-blank to do meaningless workfare, who was given endless sanctions by the Department for Work and Pensions (DWP). He never turned his heating on, survived on the cheapest canned food from Lidl, and nearly got frostbite in February 2015.

We heard stories of 'revenge evictions' i.e. tenants thrown from their homes for having the temerity to complain about faults and poor conditions. We were given examples of the poor being moved from London and offered places outside the capital, a species of social cleansing. And it was impossible not to sense the echo from some fifty years back when Ken and colleagues made *Cathy Come Home*, although this was something we never talked about.

Breaking the stereotype, we heard that many of those attending the foodbanks were not unemployed but the working poor who couldn't make ends meet. Zero-hour contracts caused havoc to many, making it impossible to plan their lives with any certainty and leaving them bouncing between irregular work and the complexity of the benefit system.

Another significant group we spoke to in the foodbanks

were those who had been sanctioned (i.e. benefits stopped as punishment, which could be from a minimum of a month to three years) by the DWP. Some of the stories were so surreal that if we had them in the script they would undermine credibility; like the father who was sanctioned for attending the birth of his child, or a relative attending a funeral, despite informing the DWP of the reasons. Literally millions have been sanctioned and their lives, and that of their children, thrown into desperation by a simple administrative decision. Criminals are treated with more natural justice, and the fines are often less than what benefit claimants lose when hit by a sanction.

This led us to another very important group of people who risked their jobs to help us: workers inside the DWP who spoke to us on an anonymous basis and were disgusted by what they had been forced to carry out in relation to sanctions. One worker in a Jobcentre showed me a print-out that showed how many sanctions he and his colleagues had given out, together with a covering letter from his senior manager, stating that only three 'job coaches' had carried out enough sanctions in the past month. If they didn't carry out more sanctions they would be threatened with the Orwellian sounding PIP, 'Personal Improvement Plan'. For the record, let me address those senior managers of the DWP and their political bosses who have given evidence before the UK and Scottish Parliaments stating that there are no targets for sanctions. You are brazen-faced liars hiding behind legalese, and your workers know it. Specific numbers might not have been given, but clear demands and 'expectation' was implicit and they were forced to get the numbers up.

Food. Heat. House. The basics, from time immemorial. We knew in our gut this film had to be raw. Elemental.

There were endless possibilities. The characters could have been similar to the young people in Nuneaton scrambling around, hovering over homelessness on zero-hour contracts. They could have been disabled, as we found out from experts the disabled have suffered on average six times more than any other group from the Government raft of cuts, a truly staggering scandal. Many of those sanctioned have been psychologically vulnerable, suffering from depression and other mental illnesses. In the memorable words of one civil servant, the easy targets were 'low hanging fruit' which perhaps could be the title of another poignant ballad to join Billie Holiday's.

The world of benefits is complicated and changing all the time, especially with Universal Credit on the horizon. It took some figuring out. But another key group that caught our attention were those men and women who were sick or injured and who had applied for Employment Support Allowance. The medical assessments for this benefit had been subcontracted to a French company, and then in turn to an American multinational after a series of scandals. The stories we heard, and the practices revealed, were legion. One furious young doctor told me of one of his patients who was dying of cancer, could barely walk, who was deemed 'fit for work'. One day he fell at home and cut his head. The ambulance was called but he refused to get in as he was signing on the next day at the Jobcentre and feared a sanction that would stop his benefits. He died about three months later. What needless misery and humiliation was caused to this older man in his last days.

All of these people deemed fit for work are forced to spend 35 hours a week looking for work. In some parts of the country there were as many as 40 people for each job advertised. One academic informed me that over the course of the last Parliament there was roughly a variation of 2.5 to 5 claimants for every job advertised. Sisyphus came to mind.

Daniel Blake and Katie Morgan are not based on anyone we met. Scripts can't just be copied and transported from the foodbank or the dole queue. Dan and Katie are both entirely fictional, but they were infused with all of the above and more. They were inspired by the hundreds of decent men, women and their children who shared their intimate stories with us. Faces of articulate intelligent people now come to mind, frightened people, older people tormented by the complexity of the system and new technology (many of the staff within the Jobcentres told us they would like to have helped more but were prevented from doing so by managers obsessed with reducing 'footfall'), young people who had lost hope far too early, some I remember trembling with anxiety as they tried to summarise their predicament, and many doing their best to maintain their dignity caught up in something misnamed as welfare which had all the hallmarks of purgatory. And yes, you opportunist, sanctimonious, commissioning producers of the crass benefits TV programmes fanning hatred and promoting ignorance, there were some drinkers and addicts with chaotic lives and odd tattoos.

There has always been a vicious streak of State bullying in our society when it comes to treating the vulnerable. All we have to do is remember the workhouses of the 19th century that insisted on splitting up mothers and fathers from their children just to make sure the gruel was tempered by sufficient cruelty.

The Rev Joseph Townsend, an 18th century vicar, summed it up. 'Hunger will tame the fiercest animals,' he wrote. 'It will teach decency and civility, obedience and subjection… it is only hunger which can spur and goad the poor on to labour.'

Plus ça change…

# I, Daniel Blake

*Screenplay*

## 1. WORK CAPABILITY ASSESSMENT

Voices against black. Impatience and exasperation growing as an assessor (female) goes through an assessment with a claimant (male) for Employment and Support Allowance (ESA). Sense of this having gone on for a long time... for both sides.

> ASSESSOR
> Can you walk more than 50 metres unassisted by another person?

> DAN
> Yes.

> ASSESSOR
> Can you raise either arm as if to put something in the top pocket of a coat?

> DAN
> Filled this out already on your 52-page form!

> ASSESSOR
> I am having some difficulty with your eligibility... Can you raise either arm to the top of the head as if to put on a hat?

> DAN
> Told you... there is nothing wrong with my arms or my legs... You have medical records... can we talk about my heart?

15

ASSESSOR

Can you press a button, such as a telephone keypad?


DAN

Nothing wrong with my fingers either... listen you're getting further and further away from my heart...


ASSESSOR

Can you use a pencil to make a meaningful mark?


DAN

Yes.


ASSESSOR

Have you significant difficulty conveying a simple message to strangers?


DAN

Yes... it's my fucking heart I keep telling you... but you won't listen.


ASSESSOR

Mr Blake, if you swear one more time I will terminate this assessment. [Pause, silence] Do you ever experience loss of control leading to extensive evacuation of the bowel?


DAN

Do you mean shit myself?


ASSESSOR

Yes.

DAN

No, but I can't guarantee this won't be a first
unless we get to the point...


ASSESSOR

Can you complete a simple task such as setting
an alarm clock?


DAN

Ah Jesus Christ... Yes.


ASSESSOR

Do you ever have uncontrollable episodes
of aggressive behaviour that would be
unreasonable in any workplace?...


DAN

Only if the radio is on and I am listening to
the news...


ASSESSOR

Mr Blake!


DAN

...Never had any problems with my
workmates...


ASSESSOR

Do you have any pets?


DAN

You mean like a hamster? Is that on the form?


ASSESSOR

I am trying to build up a picture of your
capacity to mobilise...

DAN

Is it on the form?


ASSESSOR

If you refuse to answer my question I will
terminate this assessment.


DAN

No, I don't have a pet! [Frustration spilling
over] Can I ask what medical qualification
you have?


ASSESSOR

I am a health care professional appointed by
the Department of Work and Pensions to
carry out assessments for Employment and
Support Allowance and I will not answer
personal questions...


DAN

Someone in the waiting room just told me
you worked for an American company... is
that a personal question too?


ASSESSOR

Our company has been appointed by the
Government... do you want to proceed with
the assessment?


DAN

I have a serious heart condition and I just
want to make sure you have the medical
qualifications to understand what's wrong...
are you a nurse or a doctor?

ASSESSOR

I am a heath care professional...

DAN

Do you know what ACS stands for?

ASSESSOR

I do not have to answer your questions...

DAN

Acute coronary syndrome... do you know
what 'atheroma' means?

ASSESSOR

I am not obliged to answer your questions...

DAN

Listen... I've had a major heart attack and
nearly fell off a scaffolding... I want to get
back to work too... now, will you please ask
me about my heart and forget about my arse
which works like a dream...

## 2. EXT. GOVERNMENT BUILDING, NORTHERN TOWN, ENGLAND

Daniel Blake (59) a compact man with a weather-beaten face
emerges through swing doors to the steps outside the building.
He is immaculately dressed for the occasion; coat, suit, shaved,
and polished shoes. His whole gait demonstrates that he is his
own man and takes pride in how he presents himself in public.
Dan takes a deep breath of fresh air. He catches sight of a security
guard by the entrance. They both look at a family some distance
away who are deeply distressed. An older man is in some distress
and is being comforted by his wife.

GUARD

How did you get on?

DAN

Fucking battleaxe...

GUARD

The number of people that come in here
sick... and leave perfectly cured...

DAN

Should call it Lourdes.

### 3. OUTSIDE DAN'S FLAT (SAME DAY)

1930s maisonettes, one floor up, flats off an open walkway.

As Dan moves along the walkway he is not best pleased about a
bag of rubbish left outside of the flat next door to his. He gives
it a poke with his foot. He has his keys out to enter his flat when
the door by the rubbish bag crashes open and a young lad in his
early twenties tumbles out. His nickname is China. He has his
earphones on, but still the pounding music can be heard; he is
half-singing to the music.

Dan indicates he should take his earphones off.

CHINA

[Too loud] Sorry Dan... in a right rush... just
got a text to go to work...

DAN

I'm not fucking deaf!

Dan still indicates he should take off the earphones. China does so.

DAN

Tell me... how was the chicken tikka masala?

CHINA

[Confusion on his face] Amazing... how did
you know that?

DAN

Because I can bloody well smell it... what
did I tell you about leaving the rubbish there,
stinking the place out?

CHINA

That lazy bastard, Piper... my flatmate... don't
know how many times I've told him... thick
as a plank. Can I dump it later? Running
late...

DAN

No! Pick it up now!

China picks it up.

CHINA

Dan... got a big favour to ask... expecting
a package... really important... they've just
changed my hours and I won't be in, will you
keep an eye out for the postman?

DAN

If you swear, no more rubbish...

CHINA

My whole future could turn on it Dan... that's
how important...

He sticks the earphones back on as the music pounds. He starts
messing with the rubbish bag, half-dancing with it to the terrible
racket to entertain Dan. Dan can't help but smile.

DAN

Bloody scamp.


#### 4. HOSPITAL (2 DAYS LATER)

EXAMINATION ROOM: Dan lies on a bed bare-chested as a cardiology technician uses an ultrasound to check his heart. An image of his heart (although indecipherable to the layperson) appears on a computer screen which the technician glances at. Sense of professional competence from the technician and Dan's vulnerability in the silence.

ANOTHER ROOM – OP DEPARTMENT: Dan is halfway through a conversation with a specialist cardiac nurse who has Dan's papers out in front of her on the desk between them.

SPECIALIST CARDIAC NURSE
You are making progress... but it was a
nasty one Dan... we'll continue with the
same dosage and rehab exercises... we'll see
if the pumping capacity can improve, and it
might... if not, we might have to consider
giving you a defibrillator... The doctor
makes a small pocket under the skin for it to
sit in - it's just a local anesthetic...

DAN
Sounds fun... what's that do?

SPECIALIST CARDIAC NURSE
Detects and treats dangerous fast rhythms...

DAN
When can I go back to work?

SPECIALIST CARDIAC NURSE
Not yet, that's for certain, depends on the
rehab... keep up the exercise, keep moving...
that builds you up... but you have to rest as
well...

DAN
Bit of a night bird... got into the habit when
looking after my Mrs before she passed
away...

SPECIALIST CARDIAC NURSE
Take a nap during the day then... good,
nourishing food, fresh fruit and veg, and avoid
stress... but you're doing great...

DAN
Thanks... you're a gem.

## 5. SAWMILL (3 DAYS LATER)

A local sawmill that services builders, joiners and furniture
makers in the area.

Dan enters the mill and passes by the noisy Stenner rip saws and
returns the waves of workers wearing ear protectors. It is obvious
that Dan is a well-known face, and popular figure.

Good banter among the workers. Dan greets a mate who leads
him through the mill to a place round the back with piles of
scrap wood. They handle little hand-size pieces that have been
kept for him which Dan puts in a small bag.

RONNIE
I kept you this Dan... look at the grain in
that... a fine piece...

DAN

[Savouring it with his thick hands] A beauty...
can't wait to get started on that... thanks
Ronnie...


RONNIE

Will they take you back at Ferguson's?


DAN

Depends on the work I suppose... you know
how it is, comes and goes... [Wave from
another worker] Hi Pete...


PETE

[Passing] How's the ticker Dan?


DAN

Marathon days are over... but I'll be fine in a
month or two...


PETE

Better keep off the viagra for a bit!


DAN

I'll keep them for you!


An older worker, Joe, who is about the same age as Dan, beckons
him over.


JOE

Dan... got to see this...


Joe shows him several beautiful planks of a distinctive wood.
Dan's eyes light up.

DAN

Haven't seen the likes of that for years...

JOE

Left over from a huge boardroom table... it was a lovely piece...

DAN

Gorgeous...

JOE

I'll have the boys drop it by... [Dan taps his arm in thanks, pause] Listen... no more jokes... are you okay?

DAN

On the mend...

JOE

Can bring your shopping round with the heavy stuff?

DAN

Thanks Joe... but it's good to be out and about... something to do...

JOE

Well give us a shout if you need anything... I mean that... you gave us all a fright...

6. DAN'S FLAT: NIGHT (SAME DAY)

The BBC *Shipping Forecast* theme, 'Sailing By', plays on the radio in the small hours, 12.45 am.

Dan sits at a table in his living room. He is in deep concentration with a small piece of wood in his hand. He polishes a delicate and quite beautiful fish carving, long and slender. He blows away the dust and examines his work. He catches sight of the late hour. The music comes to an end and the *Shipping Forecast,* with iconic names, and distinctive voice, reels off the changeable weather conditions in Viking, Forties, Cromarty, Forth, Tyne and Dogger… Sense of a nightly ritual, another day at an end.

### 7. DAN'S FLAT: MORNING (8 DAYS LATER)

Dan picks up the morning post which he takes into the living room.

Perplexed, he stares at a letter in his hand. He mouths the words to himself, once again, barely able to believe the contents. He crushes up the distinctive Government brown envelope into a ball and hurls it in the direction of the bin.

He looks at the letter again, and dials a number on the back of the letter from his mobile. (A simple, old-style mobile, not a smartphone.)

His frustration mounts as he is given a number of automated messages for the DWP and then finally he is put in a queue.

The sprightly first distinctive notes of Vivaldi's 'Four Seasons' ping from his mobile…

DAN

Shit…

He waits and waits. He has to stand up. He holds the phone to his ear as he looks out of the kitchen window.

Fragmented, sense of time passing:

SITTING ROOM: Dan dialling again. The same automated message. Once again Vivaldi assaults the ears as Dan is put in a queue.

It is an ordinary room, but tastefully furnished and very tidy. All around him are skillful, artistic carvings of different kinds of fish in all sorts of different coloured woods. There are some delicate 'mobiles' (ornaments that gently move with motion if touched), little fish carved as if in a shoal, linked up with fine fishing line, dangling and floating from the ceiling.

WALKWAY: Dan has the phone to his ear as he stares out at people passing. A dog stops to relieve itself. The owner looks around, coast seems clear, and doesn't pick it up. Dan can feel his fury mount.

> DAN
> Pick it up ya bloody clown!

The owner gives Dan the middle finger. Dan takes a breath to calm himself.

SITTING ROOM: Still Vivaldi. Dan now has the phone set up in front of him on speaker mode, and he tries to keep his patience as he carves on another little bit of wood.

The doorbell goes. The phone continues to peel out the music.

> POSTMAN
> Package for Max Million...

Dan is confused.

> DAN
> Max Million?

> POSTMAN
> [Checking] It's this address... no doubt.

> DAN
> My address! Where's it from?

POSTMAN

China… [Dan's face changes in
recognition]… are you going to sign for it or
not?

LATER: Back with his phone. Trying to control his fury
(conversation has already started after giving name and reference
number) as he at last gets through for the first time.

DAN

Do you know how long I have been on the
phone!? One hour and 48 minutes! Jesus
Christ, longer than a football match! Cost me
a fortune!

OFFICIAL

I am sorry sir but it has been very busy…

DAN

…There must be some kind of mistake… I
have a serious heart condition, still in rehab
and I have been ordered by my doctor not to
go back to work… I was receiving the benefit
fine till the assessment…

OFFICIAL

…You have only scored 12 points and you
need 15 points to obtain the benefit…

DAN

Points? Is this a game?

OFFICIAL

I am sorry sir, but according to our health
care professional you have been deemed fit for
work…

DAN

So she knows better than my doctor, a
consultant surgeon and the physio team... I
want to appeal.

OFFICIAL

That's fine... but you must first request a 'mandatory
reconsideration'.

DAN

What the hell does that mean?

OFFICIAL

It means the decision maker will reconsider
it... if he comes to the same decision, you can
then appeal...

DAN

Okay... put me down for that...

OFFICIAL

Okay sir, but you must wait till you get a call
from the decision maker...

DAN

What for?

OFFICIAL

To tell you what his decision is...

DAN

I thought it was made already...

OFFICAL

It is... but you are supposed to get the call,
before the letter...

DAN

Is he going to change his mind?

OFFICIAL

No, the call is just to discuss the decision.

DAN

But I know what it is! I've got the letter in my
hand... do you want me to read it?

OFFICIAL

But he should have called you first...

DAN

But he didn't...

OFFICIAL

But he should have...

DAN

Unless we have a time machine... we're kind
of stuck with that, do you not agree?

OFFICIAL

He has to call you first sir...

DAN

Okay, can you put him on the phone so I
don't waste more time?...

OFFICIAL

I can't do that sir.

DAN

Where is he?

OFFICIAL

He will give you a call back when he can sir.

DAN

When?

OFFICIAL

I don't know sir...

DAN

Are you trying to give me another heart
attack?

OFFICIAL

No sir.

DAN

Listen... I have no savings, no income, and no
pension... Is there a number I can phone for
some advice?...

OFFICIAL

0345 608 8545...

Dan notes it down with his pencil.

DAN

Thanks... Shit!! That's the number I am
on now! Going in bloody circles! Have you
another number?

OFFICIAL

All the information is online sir...

DAN

I can't do computers... can you just give me a
helpline and I'll jot it down?...

> OFFICIAL
>
> I'm sorry sir... we are digital by default. You
> have to go online.

> DAN
>
> Just between the two of us... man to man...
> do you have the number there in front of
> you?...

> OFFICIAL
>
> All the information is online sir...

> DAN
>
> Am I speaking to a human being or a
> machine?

## 8. JOBCENTRE (NEXT DAY)

Dan approaches the Jobcentre.

INSIDE: Dan enters. It is intimidating. A security guard
approaches, while the floor manager, standing close by, deals
with another claimant in no-nonsense terms; a sense of tension
pervades the place.

> GUARD
>
> [To Dan] You shouldn't be here without an
> appointment sir...

> DAN
>
> Spent a fortune on the phone... just thirty
> seconds with someone please for a bit of
> advice...

The guard reluctantly lets Dan pass then turns to deal with
someone else.

The floor manager fires off some information quickly to Dan after his questions which we don't hear. Cold and sharp.

> FLOOR MANAGER
> …One last time, quite simple… on the one hand… [holding up his right hand] … 'Job Seeker's Allowance'… only for those able and ready to work… but if you are ill you have to apply for [holding up left] 'Employment and Support' and get an assessment carried out…

> DAN
> I have, but they knocked me back…

A very harassed mother, Katie (28), with two children, a girl aged 11, and a young boy aged 9, rush past them in the background, with the mother dragging the reluctant boy along behind her.

> FLOOR MANAGER
> If you have been deemed fit for work your only option is Job Seeker's Allowance, or proceed with the appeal on Employment and Support… your choice…

> DAN
> Okay, can you give me a form to apply for Job Seeker's, and an appeal form for Employment and Support?…

> FLOOR MANAGER
> You have to apply online sir…

> DAN
> Sorry, I can't do that…

FLOOR MANAGER
That's how it is sir, or phone the helpline...

DAN
Listen... I can build you a house, but I've
never ever touched a computer...

FLOOR MANAGER
We are digital by default...

DAN
Well, I'm pencil by default... what happens if
you can't do it?

FLOOR MANAGER
There is special number if you have been
diagnosed as dyslexic...

DAN
Can you give me it?... I'm dyslexic with
computers...

Voices are raised at the far corner of the office. The floor
manager's attention is now elsewhere.

FLOOR MANAGER
You will find it online sir... I must ask you to
leave now if you have no appointment...

Dan flounders.

The floor manager nods at the security guard to go and check
the situation at the far end of the office.

DAN
Excuse me... just feeling a bit dizzy... can you
give me a second?...

Ann, an older job coach is concerned for him and approaches.

                    ANN
            Why don't you take a seat?

The floor manager is annoyed at her intervention.

Dan sits down. Ann moves to a water container for staff, pours
a little water into a paper cup and offers it to Dan. She gets a
filthy look from the floor manager for her gesture.

                    ANN
            Are you okay? You look a bit pale...

                    DAN
            I'll just need a minute... all this jargon's a
            bit confusing... somebody must have made a
            mistake... going round in circles...

The floor manager indicates that Ann should get back to her desk.

                    ANN
            Back to the grindstone...

As Ann walks back to her desk to serve someone Dan can hear
raised voices further down the office.

Sheila, a job coach in her mid-twenties, stands at her desk. She
confronts Katie, the mother, who stands beside her daughter
Daisy, and son Dylan. The tension rises, but the details cannot
yet be heard.

Dylan has a little ball and keeps bouncing and dropping it to
add to the chaos.

The tension attracts everyone's attention, including the floor
manager, security guard, Dan and Ann at a nearby desk.

The security guard comes up to Katie and leads her away despite
her protests. Sheila follows so she can join the floor manager to
support him. The action now plays out in front of Dan and other
members of the public waiting to sign on.

KATIE

I demand to speak to a manager!... I can
explain... please... [to boy] Dylan! Stop it!
[He doesn't, she grabs his arm but he shakes
her off] Stop it now!! Dylan! I can't think!

SHEILA

...You were thirty minutes late for your
appointment and I must ask you to leave...

The security guard tries to lead her away but she resists. Katie
spots the floor manager and appeals to him.

KATIE

How can you let her do this?! My first time in
the city... the bus driver gave me the wrong
stop... I ran the whole way here dragging my
kids behind me... please, it is just a mistake!

FLOOR MANAGER

You have a duty to be here on time...

KATIE

It's over the top!... [Pointing at Sheila] She's
referred me for a sanction! No money for a
month! If it was just me... but I've got two
kids! Dylan, stop it!!... We've just arrived
from London... please, you can't do that...
I've got nothing... [Totally distraught,
looking around] Jesus... I can't believe this...

[To floor manager] I'm not lying! I don't know the routes... got lost!... Please sir... I don't mind waiting... I'll wait all day...

DAISY

We ran the whole way!

FLOOR MANAGER

You have to leave the building please... the decision maker will send you a letter...

KATIE

A four-week sanction, for a few minutes late?! I can't believe it...

FLOOR MANAGER

You can apply for hardship allowance with children...

KATIE

[Desperation mounting] My kids start school tomorrow!... This can't be happening... I can't believe it... I'm begging you... please... [looking around] I don't know anybody here... Ah God, what's going on?

Dan can't bear it. He jumps up.

DAN

Jesus Christ! [To those waiting] Who's next in the queue? [Two indicate] Do you mind if this girl signs on before you?

VOICES

On you go... not at all... Give her a break!

DAN

[To officials] There you go… problem
sorted… [To Sheila] Why don't you go back
to your desk, let her sign, and do your job
which our taxes paid for! Bloody disgrace!

FLOOR MANAGER

Why don't you just shut your mouth and mind
your own business? Get out of here!

DAN

Did you listen to her?… She made a mistake,
a few minutes late… she's got two young
kids… what's wrong with you people?

SECURITY GUARD

[Grabbing Dan's arm] You, out!

DAN

Get your hands off me!

Ann watches the whole show with disgust but can't say anything.
The manager of the whole centre comes out to watch but doesn't
intervene.

KATIE

[To floor manager] Please sir… I don't want
any problems… I swear it was a mistake and
I'll never be late again… I've just moved
here… I've only twelve quid left… [opening
her purse]… and two kids to feed!

Some change bounces on the floor adding to her humiliation.
Dylan bounces the ball even harder so that it bounces from the
floor so hard it ricochets up to the ceiling.

KATIE

Dylan! For Christ sake!

FLOOR MANAGER

Get them out of here...

DAN

I'm going nowhere!

FLOOR MANAGER

Call the police...

DAN

Just tell me this... what good is this doing
anybody? Just let the girl sign on and we can
all go home... [Catching sight of the senior
manager at the door] Heh, are you in charge
here? A little common sense please...

Katie sinks to a seat in desperation as someone gives her back
her dropped change. Dylan bounces the ball even harder. He
seems oblivious to the chaos. Katie puts her head in her hands as
Dan and the security guard are still face to face. Daisy sits down
beside her and puts on her earphones.

The guard grabs Dan's arm.

DAN

Get off me!!! [To senior manager again]
Can you move your arse and sort this out...
[pulled] or have you been stuffed?!

FLOOR MANAGER

Get out or we call the police.

DAN

Call the police. What's wrong with you
clowns?

Ann [the older job coach] moves up beside Sheila [younger job coach] as she confronts the misery.

                    ANN
          Terrific... another sanction... top of the
          league.


## 9. CITY CENTRE AND STREET TO KATIE'S FLAT (SAME DAY)

Dan, Katie and the kids walk along various streets.

Dan helps her carry a few plastic bags. It is obvious they have been talking.

Katie has to keep stopping to wait for Dylan.

He is hyperactive and turns everything into a game. He swings round a pole, pounds the sides of a bus shelter, and now climbs up a four-foot wall and skips along that.

They walk down a path towards the flat. He has an old stick in his hand and he runs it along the wooden slats of the fence making a racket.

LATER: OUTSIDE KATIE'S FLAT: A 1950s maisonette. (It has seen better days, but it is not a dump. It is on the first floor above a shop. It has a shared space below covered in small granite chippings; not as good as a garden, but still a luxury after London.)

Katie stares up at the flat for a moment as Dylan, for no good reason, starts filling his trousers and jacket pockets with chippings. It makes Dan smile, wondering what is going through the child's head.

                   KATIE
          [Exasperated] Dylan! Please stop. [To
          Dan] This is it... [as if geeing herself up,
          determined]... if it's the last thing I do, I

41

swear I'm going to turn this place into a home... [pause]... you can't fix a cistern can you? Driving me insane...

She half laughs at her predicament.

> DAN
> I can fix anything... apart from a shagging computer...

## 10. INSIDE THE FLAT (SAME DAY)

Dan finishes off fixing the cistern. Katie is on her mobile to her mother. As Dan finishes the job the running water cuts off to deeply satisfying silence. Katie's face lights up and she gives a grateful thumbs up to Dan which makes him smile.

She walks back to the sitting room. Dan follows, but she is still on the phone. [Her description is the exact opposite of the truth.]

> KATIE
> It's lovely mum... freshly painted... long thick curtains [none, bare windows]... all furnished... clean as a whistle... new carpet... and warm and cozy...

Dan flicks the light switch and there is no light. He examines loose handles on shaky doors, then the windows. Even a wobbly table with a loose leg. Dan and Katie catch each other's eye as her commentary contradicts his inquiry.

> KATIE
> Once we get settled and you're feeling better... we'll get you up here with Auntie May... Okay Mum... Okay... speak soon and don't worry... honestly we're doing great...

got to go... got a friend in who's helping me
unpack... yes Mum... much more friendly
than London... Okay sweetheart... I'll phone
tomorrow... bye sweetheart...

She turns off the phone. A few moments silence. She looks at Dan.

> KATIE
>
> She's not well... what's the point of worrying
> her... Don't know how I'll cope without her.

> DAN
>
> What are you doing up here Katie?

It is almost a blow.

> KATIE
>
> [Exasperation, as if to herself] Still can't
> believe it... all I did was complain about a
> leak in my child's room... it was making him
> sick... I did nothing wrong... the landlord
> kicked us out...

> DAN
>
> They can do that?

> KATIE
>
> 'Revenge eviction'... that's what they call
> it... greedy bastards can do what they want...
> we ended up in a homeless hostel waiting
> for a flat... two bloody years... but I stuck
> with it because the kids loved their school...
> just couldn't take it anymore, one room for
> everything... really bad for Dylan... even
> needed permission for visitors... good news

was they offered me a flat with a bedroom
each... bad news... miles away... here...

### DAN

They couldn't give you anything beside your
family?

She laughs at the thought.

### KATIE

London?! They're clearing out the likes of
me... too expensive...

### DAN

How are the kids taking it?

### KATIE

Broken-hearted to leave their school,
especially Daisy... her friends... her gran,...
she's furious with me... don't blame her... but
I just had to get out for Dylan... boxed in like
that...

### DAN

She'll soon make friends...

### KATIE

Had my plan... a little garden... a bedroom
each, get a part-time job... a fresh start...
[tapping a big, distinctive cardboard box
covered in tape on the table] back to my
precious books to keep me sane...

### DAN

Were you at college?

KATIE

Open University… screwed up at school, a
second chance it was… till it all fell apart in
the hostel… [looking round] now look at
me…

She dumps the books in the corner.

KATIE

[As if pushing herself on, quietly] But I won't
give up… I can't.

Dan is touched by her fragility, and determination. He tries the
electric switch again.

DAN

Short circuit. Bloody freezing in here…
where's the fuse box?

Katie shakes her head. She is humiliated. She can't say.

DAN

What's wrong Katie?

She picks up a candle.

KATIE

Nothing on the meter… I bought the
kids some nice clothes for their first day at
school… wiped me out… thought I'd get paid
tomorrow…

Dan feels for her. He checks the shaky door on its hinge.

DAN

I'll bring my tools round… give this place the
once over…

A moment between them. Katie nods gratefully.

OUTSIDE: Dan walks off.

INSIDE: Katie carries a bucket of dirty water from cleaning the windows into the kitchen. She finds a twenty-pound note on the table, with a rough, handwritten note. 'For the electric. Here's my number. Dan.'

She sits down and stares at the big clumsy letters, written in pencil.


## 13. CHINA'S FLAT (NEXT DAY)

Dan, holding the package that came by post, pounds on the door of neighbouring flat. Another bag of rubbish is sitting there too.

A dopey looking China answers the door.

> DAN
> Max Million! My address! China! What the
> fuck is in the box?!

> CHINA
> Dan... don't jump to conclusions...

> DAN
> And how were the kebabs?

> CHINA
> Kebabs... how do you do that?

> DAN
> Nostradamus! [Kicking the rubbish]Fucking
> rubbish, pick it up! [China does so quickly]...
> And get out of my way so I can dump this
> too... I want to see what's inside this box.

Dan marches past him into the flat. China sneakily lays the rubbish back outside again before closing the door.

INSIDE: Dan, China, and his flatmate Piper [a sidekick to China, with an instinct to repeat that he tries to control but can't quite suppress] sup a cup of tea as China carefully opens, then triumphantly pulls the first spectacular pair of trainers from the box which contains about a dozen pairs.

China examines them briefly and then is beside himself, dancing around with a pair on his hands. He's so hyper with delight he does fake kung fu on Piper with the trainers still on his hands as he shouts in delight.

CHINA

Top notch!

PIPER

Fuck off... I've got brittle bone disease...

CHINA

My arse! [To Dan] Got a test for you Dan...

China gets a single, pristine shoebox from a cupboard, and places it in front of Dan.

CHINA

Go on... open it.

PIPER

On you go, open it.

China gives him a filthy look on his near repetition.

Dan takes out an identical pair of trainers to the ones that arrived in the post from China.

CHINA

What's the difference?

Dan examines them.

DAN

Look the same to me...

CHINA

Bang on brother...

PIPER

Spot on...

CHINA

The difference is this one cost me hundred
and fifty quid on the high street...

PIPER

Cost me a hundred and fifty quid! You still
owe me!

CHINA

...And I'm going to sell these for 80 quid...

DAN

Cheap counterfeits... to my fucking address...
have the Chinese mafia or customs at my
door... what a brass neck...

CHINA

Dan... Dan... not counterfeit... from the
same factory as these... exactly the same
quality... continuation of the same run... you
don't believe me... I'm going to bring back

these [counterfeit] to the shop where I bought
these [original] put them in the same box,
do a swap... say they are too big... get me
money back... and I promise they won't know
the difference... I'll use these [holding up
originals] as the show pair, and sell these on
the street... a service to the public.

PIPER

It's genius man...

DAN

How did you manage this?

CHINA

I know a wee guy in Guangzhou who works
in the factory... [looking at Dan's incredulous
face] you don't believe me... Piper?

PIPER

It's true Dan, Guangzhou... yapping every
night...

CHINA

Come in tonight for some grub... I'm going
to speak to him on Skype... [Dan's confusion]
On the net... costs me nothing...

DAN

He speaks English?

CHINA

Can't understand a fucking word he says...

PIPER

Not a word...

CHINA

But he's keen…

PIPER

So keen…

CHINA

Fuck's sake, like living with a parrot! [To
Dan] He's football mad… I just shout out
the name of the football clubs and he nearly
comes in his pants… Then we do the deal by
emails and I send him money by PayPal… and
he sends me the packages by post…

DAN

Me you mean…

CHINA

Honestly meant to ask you Dan… I get them
sent to different mates… small packages, not
to attract attention, usually get through…

PIPER

Think about it… is the Chinese State going to
do someone for ten pairs of trainers? Waste of
resources.

DAN

Is this your legal representative on
international finance? [But intrigued]
China… how did you get to know him?

CHINA

If there's a will…

PIPER

[Interjecting] There's a way...

CHINA

[Pointing to his package]... From this little
package Dan... to my own container on a
ship... how many pairs of trainers in that eh?
I'm going to manage my own consortium
Dan...

PIPER

He's serious... and I'm right behind him.

DAN

Amazing... I'll be able to tell my mates I
knew you both before you were arrested.

China puts his hands inside the trainers as if they were gloves.

CHINA

China... [smelling the leather] the future!
I'm sick of it Dan... No more shit from that
warehouse... know what the bastards did this
morning?... Called me at 5 30 in the morning,
we unpacked one truck, took 45 minutes... and
sent me home... paid me three pounds ninety
seven shagging pence! Worse than fucking
China... at least they get a 16 hour shift...

PIPER

And end up suicidal, jumping out of
windows...

CHINA

But they have nets to catch 'em! The Red

Army marches on!... [Martial art blows on
Piper with the trainers as gloves] Kung fu!!!
Fuck you!! How do you do!!

PIPER

My bones!... Not joking man!

CHINA

[Still on the attack] Not joking Piper man!
[Stopping, to Dan] I'm going to make it big...
I'm serious. [Afterthought] Do you want to be
my driver?

Dan nearly chokes on his tea.

DAN

Be your driver... can't even dump the rubbish.

14. CITY CENTRE (SAME DAY)

LIBRARY: Dan walks into a modern library which is very busy.
Big, glass windows and an impressive lift rising up through the
centre of the building.

UPSTAIRS: By the computer banks; each of the sixty seats are
taken. Dan is next in the queue and feels intimidated by the
competence of so many typing away. He gets a chance to speak
to a busy librarian.

DAN

Sorry to bother you. I need to apply for Job
Seeker's Allowance. Can anyone help me
do it with one of these contraptions on the
interweb?

LIBRARIAN

I have a cancellation in three hours... but we
don't have the staff to help...

                            DAN
              I'll be back, give it a go.

CITY CENTRE: Dan has time to kill. He wanders among
the crowd. If decent weather he might sit on a bench by the
monument watching the world pass by. If raining, he will take
shelter under the arch of the Central Arcade. He checks his
watch and heads off.

LIBRARY: Dan now sits, and is facing a computer, and may
as well be confronted with Egyptian hieroglyphics. He asks a
harassed librarian a question as she whizzes by carrying books.

                        LIBRARIAN
              Grab the mouse...

Dan's face is blank so she points to the mouse. He grabs the
mouse.

                        LIBRARIAN
              Run it up the screen.

Instead of running it up the screen he physically picks up the
mouse and runs that up the screen like a child might do with
a toy car.

                        LIBRARIAN
              Not quite...

She takes the mouse and runs the cursor up to the right spot.

                        LIBRARIAN
              You're now on the Google icon... type in Job
              Seeker's... I'll be back if I can...

And she's off, as Dan stares down at the keyboards, and then around him, like a drowning man.

                              DAN
             Grab the mouse... [To his reflection in the
             screen] I could get arrested for that...

LATER: A helpful girl in a school uniform stands over Dan. She helps him place the cursor in the appropriate box he now has to fill in. He nods gratefully as she heads off.

Dan tries to type in his name, jabbing the keys slowly with his big, stubby fingers, struggling to find each letter.

                              DAN
             [Embarrassed to another student] Excuse me,
             how do you get that bit [pointing to it on
             screen]?

                           STUDENT
             The cursor...

                              DAN
             Good fucking name for it... [pointing on
             screen again] to go down the ways...

The student tries to move the cursor down.

                           STUDENT
             It's frozen...

                              DAN
             Can you defrost it?

The student stares at Dan to see if he is taking the piss.

STUDENT

Timed out man…


OUTSIDE THE LIBRARY: Dan looks defeated as he takes some fresh air at the top of the library steps. He checks his watch.


### 15. OUTSIDE AND INTO JOBCENTRE (SAME DAY)

Dan approaches the Jobcentre and catches sight of the security guard just outside the door giving directions to an older woman. Dan takes advantage to skip inside.

He spots Ann sitting at her desk without a client. She notes his discomfort and beckons him over.

LATER: Dan is at one of the computer terminals that clients can use. Ann sits beside him, and for sake of speed leans across and types in the information he gives her for Job Seeker's Allowance.


ANN

National Insurance number?


Dan rattles through it as Ann types at speed.


ANN

You have to get this application in or you'll never get the process started…


Someone marches in behind them.


OFFICE MANAGER

[To Ann] I want to see you in my office now!


ANN

Just give me 30 seconds… last question.

OFFICE MANAGER

Immediately!

Dan can see her swallow her fury as he marches off but turns to see if Ann has obeyed.

DAN

Ah Christ... I've got you into trouble now...
I'm really sorry...

ANN

It's me that's sorry...

He watches her now disappear into the office. He stares at the form in front almost done. So close, so far. He tries to continue but presses the wrong button, and the form disappears.

He picks up the mouse in frustration.

DAN

[Holding the mouse to his mouth as if a
telephone] Come back here you bastard!

Now back to square one.

16. CHINA'S FLAT: NIGHT (SAME DAY)

Piper, with a concentrated face, makes his way from the kitchen carefully balancing three enormous mugs of tea and a snack on a tray as he makes his way to Dan and China at China's computer screen in the sitting room.

PIPER

Only one Wagon Wheel [big chocolate
biscuit] left Dan... but I've cut into four, but
you can have two pieces seeing there's only
three of us and you're the host...

Dan looks at him to see if he is taking the piss. He isn't. Dan nods gratefully.

China speaks to his Chinese contact who does his best with his decent but accented English to talk about the Premier League. The latter is a passionate lad. The whole set-up amazes Dan as he studies the image.

CHINA
Right... Barclays Premier League... here's the big question Stanley...

DAN
[Incredulous] Did he just say Stanley?

PIPER
He did, Stanley from Guangzhou.

DAN
Are you guys winding me up?

PIPER
[Serious] Not our style Dan, no way.

CHINA
Can you hear me Stanley?... Favourite player in the Premier?

STANLEY
Charlie Adam, Stoke City.

They burst out laughing.

PIPER
Stoke City! Charlie Adam?!

CHINA

Taking the piss!! How do you say that in
Chinese?!

PIPER

Agüero! A different class man...

STANLEY

No no Agüero, always injured...

CHINA

Hazard from Chelsea!

STANLEY

No no, fall over too much... Charlie Charlie!!
No big money. Sterling for City, fifty-seven
million!! Lallana, Liverpool, twenty-five
million! Stupid Gringos! Charlie Adam!
Charlie!! Only four million!! [Thumbs up] ...
No big ego, but big big heart, team man... fan
man, and big big left foot! Whacko!

CHINA

He's as slow as a donkey...

STANLEY

Quick brain... Ball fly faster than Gareth
Bale... goal against Chelsea from own half.
[Demonstrating with hand, huge long shot in
parabola, whistling] Goalllll!!!!!! [He breaks
into song adopted by Stoke fans] 'Swing
low... sweet chariot... coming for to carry me
home...'

The lads are pissing themselves.

DAN

He's not in China... he's down the road at the takeaway!

CHINA

Okay Stanley, okay okay okay enough with the talent show... I'll email you with my best price... top price... I'll see how I get on selling the ones I've got... okay, I'll let you know...

STANLEY

Best price! No bullshit! Remember Charlie Charlie, value for money... If no best price... no more trainers... no more business, no more talk... no more [he's off again] 'Swing low sweet chariot...'

CHINA

He's fucking hilarious...

PIPER

Hilarious.

LATER: Frivolity has calmed, and now the clicking of the computer keyboard. China has Dan by his side and he rattles through helping him fill in his Job Seeker's Application. It has all been done in a flash. Piper is at the other side of the room.

PIPER

I was just thinking... [it stops them all for a second] see earlier... think I got mixed up Dan... you're the guest... I'm the host...

DAN

Doesn't matter Piper... I got the extra bit of Wagon Wheel...

CHINA

Right Dan... Check your National Insurance
number... [Dan peers in and nods] ... press
that button there... send!

Dan's outstretched index finger hovers, gently taking aim,
action, bingo.

DAN

[Amazed] Been days trying to do that...

CHINA

Hey... Bill Gates! Job Seeker's done, but don't
know why the hell you are applying for that
after a heart attack... those bastards will give
you another...

China then prints off a form for him.

CHINA

And there's your appeal form for Employment
and Support... [handing it to him] but you
can't appeal till they carry out a mandatory
reconsideration...

Dan is stunned.

DAN

[Staring at the form] Is that it?... They could
have just given me one... [snapping his
fingers] like that?

CHINA

They'll fuck you around Dan... I'm warning
you... make it as miserable as possible... no
accident... that's the plan... I know dozens
who have just given up...

## 17. STREETS TO KATIE'S FLAT (NEXT DAY)

More mind-numbing Vivaldi over images of Newcastle.

Dan walks along the roads and shop fronts carrying a bag of tools. He stops occasionally for a breather on the steeper streets, taking advantage of low walls or railings. His progress is peppered with his battle with bureaucracy below...

Above the images, we have more Vivaldi and dialling sounds.

Another street. Dan, toiling, walks along.

> VOICE OF OFFICIAL
> I have a note on screen sir that you are awaiting a call from the decision maker...

> DAN
> Jesus! Fifty-five minutes waiting to hear this again!! [Exasperated] Am I stuck in a time warp?

> VOICE OF OFFICIAL
> You can't proceed to the appeal or the mandatory reconsideration till you have the call from the decision maker...

> DAN
> Will you tell him to phone me now!... I have no income... no pension... and I've still got the bedroom tax!

> VOICE OF OFFICIAL
> I'll make a note on screen sir...

> DAN
> Can you not just pass him a note? Stick it in his hand...

VOICE OF OFFICIAL
This is a call centre sir...

DAN
Where is the decision maker?!

VOICE OF OFFICIAL
I have no idea sir...

DAN
What is his name?

VOICE OF OFFICIAL
I don't have that information.

DAN
Easier to find the Loch Ness fucking
monster... Does this lazy sod actually exist?

VOICE OF OFFICIAL
May I warn you sir that this call is being
recorded. We will not tolerate aggressive
language and I am terminating this call.

## 18. KATIE'S FLAT (SAME DAY)

SITTING ROOM: It is obvious that Katie has made enormous efforts to tidy the place up and turn it into a home. Dan works on the loose door. From the corridor there is the monotonous repetitive sound of a ball bouncing against the wall.

Daisy, at some distance, reading a book, wrapped up in a blanket on the sofa, [still very cold] just watches Dan as he tightens up door hinges, handles etc. They occasionally catch each other's eye but Dan doesn't force things. Katie is cooking, sounds of her moving.

DAN

    Smells good…

Daisy just looks back to her book. Sound of a pump action screwdriver tightening up long screws. She is curious and looks up.

Dan moves to the door, curious about the sound. At the bottom of the stairs Dylan is bouncing the ball first to the ground and then against the wall in a continuous rhythm without changing.

DAN

    Dylan… do you want a shot at the
    screwdriver?

He doesn't even look up. He continues to bounce maniacally. It looks disturbing.

Dan needs a new tool. On the wall above his toolbox Dan notices a big sheet of white cardboard that has been stuck on the wall. It is a going away message from all of Dylan's mates at school, and the entire piece is covered with the memorable little handprints of 7-year-olds with names of his classmates underneath each print and a 'Good Luck Dylan' title at the top. Dylan's handprint is in the middle, with the other prints circling round it. Dan studies it for a moment.

DAN

    I like that Dylan… is that your hand in the
    middle?

Still no answer as he continues with the ball.

DAN

    Do you know what kills more people…
    coconuts, or sharks?

Still no reaction. Dan returns to the living room.

Daisy is still with her book. Same rhythmic sound of the ball.

> DAISY
>
> He started doing it in the hostel... drove us
> mad in one room...

Dan continues to work away.

> DAN
>
> Why's he do it?

> DAISY
>
> He's missing his friends... that's what I
> think... he does it when he's angry... people
> never listen to him... so why should he listen
> to them?

> DAN
>
> Can't blame him then eh? [Pause] And how
> are you Daisy?

> DAISY
>
> I'm cold... that's what I am.

She goes back to her book.

Dan checks the door, and it feels firm to the touch.

> DAN
>
> Daisy... will you do me a favour?

He holds up a measuring tape. She stares at it.

> DAN
>
> Would you mind measuring up the
> windowpanes in your room?

She studies him and puts down her book.

> DAISY
>
> What for?

> DAN
>
> You'll see...

She takes it, and disappears to her room. Katie glances with interest from the kitchen.

BEDROOM: Daisy and Dan are cutting a section of bubble wrap (as used for packing). They then put the bubble wrap up against the windowpanes.

> DAN
>
> No glue, nothing, just a bit of water and
> it sticks... the sun heats up the air in the
> bubbles and you can get light in too... it'll
> keep your room much warmer... you'll see
> the difference... [demonstrating, lifting up
> a corner, peering through] and you can peel
> it off quick too if you need to spy on the
> neighbours...

She almost smiles.

> DAN
>
> See that cloth in my toolbox... unwrap it...

She moves to the box and unwraps it carefully. She picks up a lovely mobile, a shoal of wooden fish dangling from fishing line attached to a delicate wooden frame. She holds them up, intrigued, as the fish waver with the movement.

> DAISY
>
> Ah... gorgeous...

DAN

Where will we hang them?

DAISY

For me?

DAN

A little present for your new room...

DAISY

Did you make these?

Dan nods and her face lights up in a huge smile.

LATER: Dining area. Dylan's eyes are alive for once. His face is
about the same level as the table. He stares at the tealight candles
placed on an old slate.

Dylan and Daisy are now seriously engaged as Katie watches
from the kitchen door. Dan has prepared an improvised heater
using two cheap terracotta plant pots, resting on two pieces of
wood above four little tealight candles.

DAN

[To Dylan] Go on... light the candles...

He strikes the match and lights up the candles. Dan first places
one smaller terracotta pot above the candles and then hands the
other bigger one to Daisy.

DAN

Stick that one on top Daisy... The candles
last about four hours... it takes a while, but
the heat rises from the hole on the top...
feel the heat here Dylan [he does so, his face
intrigued]... but it takes the chill off the air...
you'll feel the difference...

DYLAN

[Holding his hand over the hole] Wao... were you a soldier?

DAN

Much more dangerous than a soldier... a carpenter.

Katie watches too, intrigued.

KATIE

Right... grub's ready...

DAN

I'm okay... thanks anyway...

KATIE

It's ready!

She brings through three plates of food [paper plates] and lays them down on the table, plastic knife and fork, for Dan and the two kids.

DAN

Where's yours?

KATIE

Had mine earlier... just fancy a bit of fruit...

DAISY

You said that yesterday... and the day before.

Katie starts to peel the apple, avoiding Dan's eye.

DAN

Looks delicious... but a wee bit early for me...

                              KATIE
              Please Dan… it's the least I could do…

He catches a look in her eye that rocks him to the core. Silence
for a moment.

                              DAN
              Thank you Katie.

### 19. KATIE'S FLAT, BATHROOM AND STAIRS (SAME NIGHT)

Katie stands inside the bath and scrubs some crusty filth from
in between the tiles and corners that have not seen detergent in
an age. She is using a bit of rag and washing-up liquid which
doesn't make it any easier.

Two old tiles, with grout badly worn, fall from the wall and
crash into the bath.

                              KATIE
              Oh God…

It is the last straw.

Katie comes out of the bathroom which is at the foot of the
stairs carrying a bucket containing the rags, cleaning stuff and
broken tiles. She slumps onto the second last step and leans her
head against the wall.

She becomes aware of steps behind her. Daisy, in her nightdress,
is on the stairs.

                              DAISY
              It's far too late Mum… time to sleep.

Daisy sits down beside her on the step and looks at her mum.
She can see she is upset and notices her red eyes.

                    DAISY
    Oh Mum...


                    KATIE
    I've just got a terrible headache darling...
    don't worry... I'll be fine.


                    DAISY
    Do you think I'm stupid?


Daisy holds her eye and there is no hiding place.


                    KATIE
    I'm just so tired sweetheart... in my head.


Daisy wraps her arms around her and pulls her as tight as she can.


                    DAISY
    You are a brilliant mum... I'm the luckiest girl
    in the world.


It sparks Katie off again, as Daisy cradles her head down to hers.


<u>20. KATIE LOOKS FOR WORK (NEXT DAY)</u>

CHARITY SHOP: From outside we see Katie and the shopkeeper add her card for cleaning work to others in the shop window.

GEORGIAN TERRACE: Stunning and elegant Georgian terrace in a memorable crescent.

Katie walks from door to door putting her cleaning advert through the doors.

She looks worn out and takes a breather on a step while she counts out how many cards she has left.

## 21. JOBCENTRE (7 DAYS LATER)

Dan sits opposite a job coach, Sheila. She holds up a booklet and a form.

> ### SHEILA
> This is the Claimant Commitment Form...
> you must commit yourself to spending 35
> hours a week looking for work... newspapers,
> agencies, and online via the Universal Job
> Match... [indicating]... fill in the details here
> and you must prove this too...

> ### DAN
> I have been told by my doctor, not to start
> work yet...

> ### SHEILA
> You should apply for Employment and
> Support...

> ### DAN
> [Trying to control exasperation] I have, but
> been rejected by some cowboy quack and I am
> now trying to appeal...

> ### SHEILA
> Your choice Mr Blake.

> ### DAN
> No. It is not my choice... I have no other
> income...

> ### SHEILA
> You should seek independent legal advice...

DAN

And starve in the meantime?


SHEILA

We always try to respect the wishes of the
customer user. [Pushing over the document]
Do you want to sign or not?


Dan has to swallow his pride. He takes the form and signs.


SHEILA

Can I see your CV?


DAN

My CV?


SHEILA

You still don't get this Mr Blake. [Holding up
the booklet] This is an agreement between
you and the State. You can't find work
without an up-to-date CV.


DAN

No, you don't get it... I am desperate to go
back to work, but only when the doctor says
I can.


She checks her diary.


SHEILA

There is a CV workshop here on Saturday
morning 9am.


DAN

No thanks... I'll manage on my own.

                    SHEILA
No Mr Blake… this is a formal direction. You
will attend if you want to proceed with Job
Seeker's Allowance.

                    DAN
And if I don't?

                    SHEILA
You will be referred for a sanction.

                    DAN
When will I get my first payment?

                    SHEILA
In fifteen days… if you can prove to our
satisfaction you have been genuinely looking
for work…

Dan stares at her.


## 22. STREET AND INSIDE FOODBANK / CHURCH HALL (NEXT DAY)

Dan, Katie, Daisy and Dylan, lagging behind as usual, head
towards a church hall.

An enormous queue stretches round the block. Dan, Katie and
the kids walk along the side of the queue, and then turn the
corner. They walk by many more people till they get to the tail
end of the queue. Katie is pale and looks a bit dizzy, and puts
her hand up to the wall to steady herself.

                    DAN
Are you okay?

                    KATIE
Just a tummy bug…

INSIDE THE HALL: They enter. Dan stands to the side as Katie and the kids enter and make their way inside.

Dan, by the door, studies the parade of worn faces. Some look fragile and embarrassed, and others just make their way round the stalls with different types of food. The woman by the door from the foodbank is warm and welcoming as Katie hands her a voucher. (Given by a referral agency for those in need.)

Dan can see Katie and the kids make their way round. The people who run it are kind to Daisy and Dylan.

An older woman appears at the door. She looks nervous and ashamed.

> VOLUNTEER
> Come in Helen...

> HELEN
> [Embarrassed] Been before... are you sure
> there is enough?

> VOLUNTEER
> Doesn't matter... it's okay... good to see you
> again...

Dan watches her pick up a modest amount of fresh veg with her skinny hand.

> VOLUNTEER
> [To Dan] Have you come for a parcel?

> DAN
> [Crisp] No thank you.

Daisy and Dylan hover around the biscuits, and the volunteers are generous to them. Katie picks up some cereals and then moves to the section dealing with soaps, toothbrushes, toothpastes, shampoos etc. She looks humiliated, and very uncomfortable.

KATIE
[Whispered to volunteer] I'm sorry... but do you have any sanitary towels... just a few?

VOLUNTEER
I'm sorry love, we are out.

KATIE
No problem... sorry to bother you...

BY ANOTHER STALL: Katie looks anxious as she confronts a wall full of different types of tins.

VOLUNTEER
Looking for a favourite?

KATIE
I'll take anything...

The volunteer puts several tins in her bag.

KATIE
Thank you.

As the volunteer moves on, Katie spots a can with a ring pull in her bag. In a sudden impulse she snaps at it and has it opened before she realizes.

She turns into a corner by the shelves.

She can't resist the opened can. She starts scooping out the beans with her hands, wolfing down the food, oblivious to everything.

DAISY
[Screaming] Mum! What are you doing?!

Katie becomes aware of herself, hands covered in sauce, some has dripped on to her trousers, and there is some sauce over her chin. She is humiliated.

Dan runs over to her.

DAISY
Disgusting...

Daisy runs off to the other side of the hall.

KATIE
[As if frozen, unable to move] I'm sorry... I'm so sorry... didn't realize Dan, I was so... so... felt faint... [looking down at her hands] like a rat... so glad my mum can't see me...

Dan leads her over to a nearby table and chair. He takes an old fashioned hanky from his pocket and helps clean her up.

DAN
It's okay Katie... you're okay. No harm done...

She begins to sob uncontrollably. He takes her hand in support as she totally collapses.

KATIE
Dan... I'm going under... I can't cope...

DAN
You'll get through this darling... it's not your fault... you've been amazing, dumped up here on your own...

Another volunteer comes over to Katie with a mug.

                    VOLUNTEER
          It's okay love… some hot soup… you're not
          the first, believe me…

Dan catches sight of Daisy, upset too, being comforted by the
volunteer who was at the door.

Little Dylan, with an open packet of biscuits, comes over and
just stares at his mum.

                    DAN
          She'll be okay in a minute Dylan.

He just looks as he munches down a biscuit.

## 23. ROOM IN OFFICE BLOCK, CV WORKSHOP (6 DAYS LATER)

Dan, sitting at the back, studies a mixture of characters around
him. Some look competent and organized, while others look
like they could never hold down a job in their current state.
Some are lost, confused, withdrawn, and others look agitated
with addiction problems.

An energetic man in a suit presents a workshop on CVs. He has
worked his way through various headline points on a board and
is mid-flow. [Points include, Short and sharp, not a life story,
bullet points, Digital CV, Video CV, Keywords, Telling the
Truth.]

                    MANAGER
          [Holding up his hands, fingers outstretched]
          Ten seconds… ten short seconds! That's how
          much the typical employer spends flicking
          through a CV… fact. Sixty applications for

every low-skilled job... fact. For a skilled
job... it's 20 to 1. Fact. Costa Cafe advertised
eight jobs... do you how many applications
they got? Over 1,300! Fact! So what does that
mean?

                    DAN
We should all drink much more fucking
coffee.

Several burst out laughing, but Dan is not smiling.

                    MANAGER
This is serious sir... and mind your language.

                    DAN
Obviously, if you can count... means there are
not enough jobs. Fact.

The manager is not impressed. Dan notices a man in his forties
in a suit catch his eye. The latter gives him the thumbs up for
his contribution which he clearly enjoyed.

                    MANAGER
For those who live in the real world... it
means... [pointing at his presentation bullet
point] you must 'STAND OUT FROM
THE CROWD'. Get noticed, get smart!
Not enough to show you have the skills...
you have to prove how keen you are... how
determined ... if needs be, to smile hour after
hour to the customer... if not, back of the
queue... so I want you now to start drafting
your CVs and remember... these should all
be typed out in a clear font in hard copy,

with a digital version too for online... some
employers are now demanding CV videos sent
in by smartphones... so remember, short and
sharp, all the positives without exaggerating,
be realistic, and tell the truth...

LATER: Dan drafts his CV in pencil while another younger
woman beside him flashes through it on an iPad. Some lost souls
are really struggling and can hardly write. One distracted lad
makes a paper aeroplane with his A4 sheet of paper.

LATER: The manager is back in front of them.

> MANAGER
> I want everyone to read out their
> summaries... I want to see immediate
> impact... we'll go round the room, starting
> from the back...

A shy, middle-aged woman gives a few lines from her CV as the
manager genuinely encourages her.

A few fragments from other contributors too until it is Dan's
turn.

Dan has to hold his piece of paper at arm's length.

> DAN
> Sparky personality. Honest, reliable, hardly
> missed a day's work in forty years.

> MANAGER
> Very strong... good.

> DAN
> Fit as a butcher's dog, apart from a recent
> heart attack which nearly killed me that might

preclude me from working with dangerous
machinery, working with small children,
[looking up at the manager] or involves any
stressful interaction with clowns…

Some of the group are pissing themselves, but not the manager,
while others are shocked at his defiance.

OUTSIDE: Dan and the man in the suit who gave him the
thumbs up, Michael, are halfway through a conversation. Maybe
Michael is smoking.

> MICHAEL
> Don't take them on Dan… you can't beat
> them… show a little spirit and it'll whet
> their appetite… trust me, I've seen it… keep
> the head down… only way… do the CV,
> get the job search done or you'll end up in
> Poundland stacking shelves on workfare… I
> was sanctioned for six months… lost my flat,
> on the streets… don't think it can't happen…
> it can, and they don't give a toss if you drop
> dead. Comes from the top. No mistake.

> DAN
> What's your work?

> MICHAEL
> I'm an accountant.

> DAN
> What are you doing here?

He hesitates for a second.

> MICHAEL
> Had a breakdown… but I'm getting there…
> good luck Dan, I mean that.

### DAN

You too Michael.

### MICHAEL

Be careful…

His intensity shocks Dan.

### 24. SUPERMARKET (2 DAYS LATER)

A security guard monitors a screen. He is interested in someone. He moves in closer and studies the body language of a young woman.

AISLE: Katie looks very uncomfortable and stressed. She has a few items in her shopping trolley. She moves along the aisle examining the prices of various items. She looks up and down the aisle. She moves to the sanitary towels and examines the prices of various brands, and then puts them back again.

A woman leaves the aisle and disappears. Another one at the other end turns her back. Katie looks both ways and takes a breath to calm herself. She moves along a little and then grasps another pack of sanitary towels and stuffs it quickly inside her coat.

CHECKOUT: Katie's eyes glance round her nervously as she studies the face of the bored cashier scanning the half dozen items. She hands in the last item, hesitates, then catches her eye. The cashier gives her the receipt and she pays.

As she walks to the door the security guard stands in her way.

### SECURITY GUARD

Madam… we have reason to believe you have been shoplifting. Can you come with me to the office?

KATIE

[More to herself] Oh God... Oh God... I'm
sorry... [Biting her lip] Can I put it back?

OFFICE: Katie sits on a simple seat, her head bowed in shame.
On the desk in front of her are two bags of rice and a box of
sanitary towels.

At her feet are the other items she bought in plastic bags.

The security guard stands at the door. Neither say anything. But
his eyes linger over her.

Silence for a few moments. The store manager comes in and
nods at the security guard.

STORE MANAGER

Thanks Ivan... I'll take it from here.

The security guard hesitates for a second, and then leaves. An
awkward silence. Katie looks up at the manager.

KATIE

I've never done this before... what will
happen to my kids?

She is confused as the manager takes the stolen items from the
table and places them in her shopping bags. Silence between
them for a moment.

KATIE

I don't understand...

MANAGER

Neither do I... [hesitation] this is between me
and you, and nothing to do with the store...
these items have now been paid for...

The unexpected kindness is a bigger blow than any scolding. She holds her hands to her face, overwhelmed.

Katie walks to the exit. The security guard stands by the door and the panic rises in her face again. But he is smiling.

> SECURITY GUARD
> Relax... it's okay... [She is still frightened]
> You could be earning a small fortune... [a
> moment's confusion] a pretty girl like you...
> here's my number, give me a call anytime...

He holds out a yellow sticky note but she refuses to take it, her face blank. He slips it into one of the shopping bags.

> SECURITY GUARD
> My name's Ivan. I know yours... Katie.

## 25. DAN'S FLAT (2 DAYS LATER)

Little Dylan sits in a corner of the sitting room, and he polishes a rough-carved wooden fish with sandpaper; a fierce energy, his entire attention focused.

Inside the kitchen Dan and Katie prepare a meal, chopping up some food. Katie, by the kitchen door, is stunned as she watches Dylan work away on the carving.

> KATIE
> First time he has ever sat still on his
> backside... over fifteen minutes!

Dan chuckles.

> DAN
> It helps me too...

Daisy, curious, noses around the living room and looks at a few old photographs. A younger Dan with a pretty woman beside him. Then she notices something.

DAISY

What's this Dan?

She holds up a cassette and examines it. She sticks her finger in one of the round holes and turns it gently.

DAN

Are you serious? [She nods] It's a cassette...
[she is still blank] tape inside... [no
reaction]... music on it...

DAISY

[Holding it up, peering through one of the
holes] Are you joking Dan?

He chuckles and grabs an old clunky cassette player, flicks open the lid and sticks the cassette in.

DAN

Press there...

DAISY

Look at the size of the button Mum!

Dan laughs. She presses it down but it is too stiff.

DAN

Harder!

He helps her press, and it clicks down. 'Sailing By' comes on. Daisy listens, swaying gently.

                              DAN

          … It was Molly's… she recorded it off the
          radio… shipping forecast… on late every
          night… 'Sailing By'…

The music continues as Dan joins Katie in the kitchen.

                              DAN

          Good to be cooking for someone again…

Katie just smiles.

                              DAN

          How did the interviews go?

                             KATIE

          Nothing works with the school times… put
          my name down with agencies, on waiting
          lists… could clean in the mornings… let's
          see… went round the hotels too… cafes…
          walked for miles… feet killing me…

                              DAN

          I can give you a hand, pick up the kids till
          I get back to work… What about the guest
          house advert?

                             KATIE

          Man was a creep… eyes all over me.

                              DAN

          Bastard.

Dan drops all the cut up ingredients into a pot.

KATIE

Good to be cooked for.

A moment between them.

LATER: At the table. Dylan wolfs down the food and soaks up the sauce with a piece of bread. He suddenly looks up at Dan.

DYLAN

Coconuts.

It takes Dan a moment to twig what he's on about and then remembers.

DAN

Correct!

Katie smiles.

LATER: Dylan is curled up in an armchair polishing the same piece of wood. Daisy looks at a photo on the shelves.

KATIE

Is that Molly?

Dan nods. Daisy takes it down from the shelf and examines her.

DAISY

[As if to herself] Molly… like that name…
what was she like?

Dan hesitates for a second.

DAN

She was special Daisy… but not easy… she
was up, she was down… very smart, funny,

kind... a big big heart... but... [pause, but
their attention spurns him on] she said her
head was like the ocean... dead still, then
wild... never knew what was coming next...
the music helped her... but sometimes she
hit the rocks... we used to play it at night
before going to bed, help her calm down, stop
her mind racing... find sleep if she could...
'Where will we sail tonight Dan?' That was
her little joke... [Pause] Her last words to me
were... 'I want to sail along with the wind at
my back... that's all I need Dan...'

They listen in silence as Dan examines the photo for a second
and stares at her.

DAISY

Did you have any children?

DAN

[Shaking his head] I would have loved that
Daisy...

DAISY

Do you miss her?

KATIE

Daisy...

DAN

It's okay... She was crazy... hard work... but I
loved her to pieces...

DAISY

Manic depressive... [Dan is amazed] We had a
few of them at the hostel.

Daisy puts the picture back on the shelf.

IN THE KITCHEN: Katie and Dan have cleared up and Dan puts the last items away in a cupboard, quietly and methodically.

> KATIE
> Must have been hard for you Dan... Did you look after her till the end?

Dan is quiet for a moment, then nods.

> DAN
> I thought it would be a relief when she passed... I stopped and started work depending how she was... but after you've cared for someone so long... it fills up your whole life...

> KATIE
> And forget about your own?

Dan shrugs.

> DAN
> Well... it was hard to invite people back... you get kind of used to [struggling for the words] becoming private, very private... without realising...

> KATIE
> She was lucky to have you... I ended up with someone... [pause]... he wasn't a good person Dan... my mum warned me... but you can't be told at eighteen. And I did it again with Dylan's dad... a control freak.

DAN

You're young... whole life ahead of you...
once you get back to those books you'll feel
better...

KATIE

Can't bear to look at them... really upsets
me...

DAN

It'll work out... just you wait...

KATIE

We'll see.

She looks overwhelmed with it all.

DAN

We all need the wind at our back now and
again... it'll change.

### 26. DAN TRYING TO FIND WORK (NEXT DAY)

Time passing. Dan looks tired and worn out by the process.

GARDEN CENTRE: Dan hands over a handwritten photocopy
of his CV to a manager.

SUPERMARKET: He hands over another.

WAREHOUSE: An energetic manager studies Dan's CV. He
actually looks interested.

OWNER

Sick of some of those bloody young ones
not turning up, or screwing up... [Flicking
over it] I'll give you a phone... that's a lot of

experience... thanks for popping by... Harry
Edwards... that's my name...

Dan sheepishly nods his head, embarrassed by the interest.

MAIN STREET: Dan is in and out of a few shops, and then
enters a clothes shop.

INSIDE: Dan hands over his photocopied CV to a young
woman and young man in ultra trendy clothes. They take it
politely, but are bursting inside, catching each other's eyes and
feeling like kids in church trying to contain themselves.

                    DAN
        Just in case you ever need a handyman for the
        building... I can do anything...

It releases the tension and the two youngsters burst into giggles.

                    GIRL
        I'm sorry... really sorry... at first I thought
        you wanted to work as an assistant...

                    DAN
        [Not unkindly] Yeah... that would be
        funny...

As he leaves he can see the two of them in stitches. He feels
humiliated.

BACK LANE: Something to lift his spirits. He catches sight
of China and Piper working from a fold-up table covered in
trainers. A half dozen youngsters swarm round as others are
attracted by the show. He is really giving them the patter...

                  CHINA
    Quality trainers! Straight from the factorrrrry!

PIPER

Straight from the factorrrrrry!


CHINA

No middlemen!


PIPER

None at all!


China catches sight of Dan, and the latter gives him the thumbs up. China breaks out in an easy smile. Dan enjoys his vitality.


DAN

[Fist in the air] The future! Good old Stanley!


CHINA

Next time you see me... I'll need a driver!


DAN

I'm your man...


Dan waves at him and walks off.

A man shouts at him from across the road. It is Joe from the sawmill.


JOE

Dan... Dan... going down the pub tonight,
a few beers... come on down... some good
music too...


DAN

Thanks Joe... got to keep off the sauce... but
I'll pop by the mill...


Joe waves at him and walks on.

Dan's phone begins to ring and he starts fumbling in his pockets. He manages to get the phone out of the right pocket but it just stops ringing.

                    DAN
          Shit!

Dan turns into a shop doorway. He listens to the message as he tries to block out the sound of the traffic with a finger to his ear.

                    ANSWER MACHINE
          Message for Daniel Blake. This is a call from
          the DWP decision maker. You should soon
          receive a letter which states that you have
          been deemed fit for work and not entitled to
          Employment and Support Allowance. Further
          information is available online. Thank you.


## 27. DAN'S FLAT (NEXT DAY)

Dan has been opening his mail. He stares at a hefty electric and gas bill. It has red letters along the top, Final Demand. The landline phone rings. He answers.

                    VOICE
          Harry Edwards here... manager of the
          warehouse... I got a chance to go through
          all the CVs and wonder if you can manage to
          come in for an interview tomorrow?

                    DAN
          [Hesitant] I'm sorry Mr Edwards... but I have
          been told by my doctor not to go back to
          work yet... it's hard to explain...

                    VOICE
          So why did you hand in the CV?

                      DAN
       It's the only way I can get any benefits...


                      VOICE
       I studied your CV with respect! Red tape and
       bloody scroungers driving me insane... I do
       a 12-hour day and I get shit like this... stop
       wasting our fucking time and money!

He cuts off the phone. Dan feels profound shame.

## 28. JOBCENTRE (2 DAYS LATER)

Sheila the young job coach examines Dan's booklet detailing his
job search as Dan sits opposite her like a naughty child.

                      SHEILA
       Not good enough Mr Blake... how do I
       know you have been in contact with all these
       employers? Did you keep a copy letter?


                      DAN
       I walked round the town, handed in my CVs
       by hand.


                      SHEILA
Prove it.


                      DAN
How?


                      SHEILA
       Did you ask for a receipt? Take a photo on
       your mobile?

DAN

[Showing his mobile] With that? I give you
my word... that's what I did.


SHEILA

Not good enough Mr Blake... what about the
Universal Job Match online?


Dan fiddles in his pocket and takes out a slip with his computer
appointment.


DAN

I went down the library... here's my slot...
tried my best... drove me mad...


SHEILA

Not good enough... let me see your CV.


Dan hands her a copy of his photocopied CV. [Copied from
original in pencil.]


SHEILA

Did you not learn anything in the CV
workshop?


DAN

You'd be surprised.


She examines the CV with contempt.


DAN

[Holding her eye, slowly] Not good enough...


It raises her hackles.

                              SHEILA

            I'm afraid I will have to refer you to a decision
            maker for a possible sanction for four weeks…
            your payment will now be frozen… You may
            be entitled to hardship allowance if you apply.
            Do you understand?

Dan just stares at her.

                              SHEILA

            If you are sanctioned you must continue to
            look for work and sign on or you may be
            sanctioned again which is likely to be for
            thirteen weeks on the second occasion and
            thereafter up to a maximum of three years.

She hands him back his booklet.

                              SHEILA

            Would you like me to write out a referral to a
            foodbank?

Dan stares at her for several seconds, then walks out.

Fade.


## 29. STREET OUTSIDE AND INTO DAN'S FLAT
## (6 WEEKS LATER)

A second-hand furniture dealer van is outside Dan's house. Two
strong lads carry out various pieces of furniture, including the
armchair and a hefty sideboard.

China, on his way out, stops in his tracks for a moment in shock.
He spots Dan by the van.

                              CHINA
            Dan… you're not leaving are you?

DAN

Heading for the Bahamas... [momentary
surprise, then as the rolled-up carpet goes by]
sick of this stuff, need a freshen up...

China senses something. Dan looks knackered.

CHINA

Are you okay Dan?

DAN

Fine son...

CHINA

You haven't even given us a row... for leaving
out the rubbish...

DAN

I'm okay China... thanks anyway...

CHINA

If you need anything... give me a shout...

A warm moment between them.

INSIDE FLAT: The dealer notices Dan's toolbox which has the
lid up revealing his kit.

DEALER

What about these?

DAN

[Shaking his head] No chance... I'll be back
to work soon.

The dealer eyes up the mobiles still dangling down from what

is now a very empty sitting room made all the more spartan by the bare floorboards.

> DEALER
> [Touching one] Quality... how much do you want?

> DAN
> Not for sale.

The dealer hands Dan some cash which Dan checks. He is not impressed by the amount and sticks the money in his pocket.

> DEALER
> Call me if you change your mind... see you now.

He leaves and closes the door.

Dan leans up against the wall staring at his bare room apart from the mobiles and a picture of Molly. Sense of loss and emptiness strike deep.

## 30. KATIE'S FLAT: NIGHT (2 DAYS LATER)

Daisy walks through to her mum's room and jumps into bed with Katie.

Katie cuddles into her back and can feel her child shiver despite all the blankets piled up.

> KATIE
> You're freezing darling... did it keep you awake? [No answer] What's wrong love?

> DAISY
> One of the girls was making fun of my clothes...

KATIE

You look gorgeous…

DAISY

[Hesitant] Said I was sweaty and smelly…

KATIE

Don't you listen to her…

DAISY

It's true…

KATIE

Why didn't you say darling?

DAISY

You're doing your best Mum…

Katie feels ashamed.

KATIE

I'll take everything to the laundry
tomorrow… that's a promise…

Katie cuddles her tight, as her face hardens.

LATER: SITTING ROOM: Katie walks through to the sitting
room, wrapped up in a blanket. She has her phone in her hand.

She sits on the sofa and takes her purse from her bag which has
been left on the sofa. She opens it, extracts the sticky yellow
post-it, and sees the name 'Ivan' and number.

She stares down at it, one last hesitation. She gathers up her
courage and dials.

VOICE

Who's this?

KATIE

Do you remember me... the girl from the
supermarket?

SECURITY GUARD

Katie... glad you phoned.

## 31. STREET AND BAR: NIGHT (NEXT DAY)

Katie, looking her smartest, and very attractive, walks down a
busy street.

She hesitates outside a cafe. She spots the people she is looking
for inside. She builds up her courage and enters.

Through the glass front we see her approach two people. One is
Ivan, the security guard. The other is a smartly-dressed woman
in her forties who stands up politely to greet Katie and shakes
her hand.

They sit down to talk.

## 32. KATIE'S FLAT (SAME NIGHT)

Dan sits in Katie's sitting room, in his overcoat. He is working
away again on a carving. There is an improvised terracotta heater
with tealight candles on beside him.

He hears the front door open and Katie comes in.

KATIE

Thanks Dan... did they go down okay?

DAN

No problem... fast asleep. How did it go?

KATIE

A good talk... a single parent's group... had a
friendly chat with one of the mums after...

                    DAN
        Great… some good people round here…

                    KATIE
        I'll just check them…

In the hallway, Katie sees Dan out. He can sense her tension.

                    DAN
        Are you okay?

                    KATIE
        Just tired Dan… thanks a million… see you
        soon.

                    DAN
        Anytime… sleep well.

Dan heads down the one flight of stairs to the main door out to the street.

By the bottom door Dan notices an envelope lying on the ground. He bends down to pick it up. On one side he reads Katie's full name, Katie Morgan and current address. He turns it over and reads in handwriting the website address www. saffronescorts.co.uk followed by a telephone number.

Dan is stunned, and hesitates. He doesn't know what to do with the envelope. He looks up the stairs towards Katie's flat.

He puts the envelope in his pocket and leaves.

## 33. DAN'S FLAT (SAME NIGHT)

Dan uses the space of the living room, now virtually empty. He works with energy and precision as he cuts up the last of the mahogany planks over two trestles and the sawdust drops to the bare floorboards.

He finishes off making the top shelf to a simple but elegant bookcase.

His phone rings but he ignores it. It goes on to speakers and answering machine. He stops working for a second as Katie's voice comes on. (There is something gentle and vulnerable about her tone which Dan picks up on.)

> KATIE'S VOICE
> Dan… [moment's hesitation] thanks for
> coming round tonight… [A sigh]… Daisy
> woke up… she forgot to ask you something…
> she has to interview someone about their
> work for a school project… she wants to ask
> you. Is that okay? They loved your made up
> stories tonight… she said Dylan was laughing
> and laughing… [emotional]… it almost made
> me cry… Sleep well Dan… byeeee.

It gets Dan. He lays down his tool and slumps forward in his chair. He looks done in and exhausted. He takes the envelope from his pocket and reads the words again.

He knows the truth in his heart. He pinches the brow of his nose as he tries to think clearly despite the blow.

Fade.

## 34. DAN'S FLAT (A FEW DAYS LATER)

Dan has his phone to his ear as he gets through to someone.

> DAN
> Is this the number for the escort agency?

> VOICE
> I'll give you another number mate.

> DAN
>
> I hear you had a new girl starting last week.

> VOICE
>
> That's right... phone this number now and
> you'll get all the info... have you got a pen?

## 35. SUBURBAN ROAD AND FLAT (SAME DAY)

Dan walks down a street, phoning to get the house number which he repeats.

He spots the house he is looking for and walks down the short path. He rings a bell and the door lock buzzes. Dan enters and he is soon into a hallway.

He meets an ordinary looking woman in her late forties.

> WOMAN
>
> You're ten minutes early... but it's okay to go
> in...

Dan looks embarrassed and pulls out his wallet to pay.

> WOMAN
>
> No... you pay her inside... [indicating]... first
> door on the right... she's waiting... excuse
> me...

She disappears into the kitchen and Dan can hear the distant sound of a radio and cooking utensils on the go.

Dan moves towards the door. He looks very uncomfortable and hesitates.

At last he knocks.

> KATIE'S VOICE
>
> Come in...

INSIDE: The room has been tarted up for purpose.

Dan, in an instant, takes in Katie's skimpy lingerie under a semi-transparent gown. Katie is stunned for a second, like a body blow. She suddenly crosses her arms across her chest, as if confronting her father.

> DAN
>
> [Gently] Katie... this is not for you... I want to help...

> KATIE
>
> [Whispered] You shouldn't see me like this... this is something... separate... cut off... Please get out...

> DAN
>
> Katie... listen... I just couldn't talk to you in your house...

She can't bear it. Katie swirls round, grabs her coat from a hook and barges past him. He follows her out.

> DAN
>
> Katie! I've got to speak to you... I was so confused... didn't know what to do... Please...

But she's off, scurrying out the door, along the corridor, then out into the street.

> DAN
>
> Katie!

Dan follows at speed.

DAN

Katie! Please listen to me!

But she is away, with Dan trying to catch up. A few yards along
she turns first right down the lane, and with Dan still following
she turns again, just to get away, but it brings her behind the
building into a cul-de-sac, full of bins and rubbish, and she's
trapped in a filthy corner.

She turns to face Dan who is now opposite her. Lit rooms from
the back of the houses shed a little light. She is raw, exposed,
resigned, and now holds his eye.

They are both devastated as they look at each other. Dan
struggles to control himself.

DAN

I came to tell you... [almost cracking]... I
made you a bookcase...

She starts to shake her head.

KATIE

Don't... don't say anymore...

DAN

For your books Katie...

KATIE

I can't bear it... I beg you...

He doesn't know what to say, what to do, where to look. He
looks above him and he lets out a groan.

DAN

Jesus Christ... this is breaking my heart!

He suddenly grabs her in a clasp as he might do to a daughter. She puts her arms around him too.

After a few long moments they calm a little. She speaks quietly into his ear as she still holds him tight.

KATIE
You know Dan… no words…

He shakes his head, and tries to swallow a sob.

DAN
Fuck…

Another long moment.

KATIE
[Slowly, quietly] I've got three hundred quid in my pocket… I'm going to buy the kids fresh fruit… not past the sell-by date… if you can't deal with this, I can't see you anymore, because I'm going back in there… back in now… [struggling to get the words out, almost cracking again] if you speak to me… if you show me any more love… I'm going to break… don't break me Dan… it's hard enough.

She grips him tighter and he responds.

At last she releases him and they separate. She drifts past him like a ghost.

Dan leans up against the wall, and sinks to his hunkers as he tries to control profound grief that overwhelms him.

Fade.

## 36. CITY STREETS

A sense of time having passed. (7 days later.)

Dan trudges along a street with a bunch of the same photocopied CVs in his hand. He folds them up and pops them into the letter box of a few businesses or pubs.

In another street, he goes from shop to shop, barely pausing as he hands over his CV.

He stands on a corner, dispirited, not certain which direction to take. He waits and waits. Traffic passes in front of him.

## 37. JOBCENTRE (NEXT DAY)

Dan looks much the worse for wear, and he has not shaved in a week. His shirt is crumpled and his shoes are scruffy too.

He now has to sign on again but this time he sits opposite the friendlier, older job coach, Ann.

She examines his Claimant Commitment Form and her confusion grows as she flicks through a few more pages.

> ANN
> I'm a bit confused... what jobs have you
> applied for?

> DAN
> It's a grand farce isn't? [Noticing] Your
> friendly name tag on your chest... 'Ann' ...
> opposite a sick man, looking for non-existent
> jobs which I couldn't do anyway... wasting
> my time, employers time, your time... all it
> does is humiliate me... grind me down...
> is that the point... get my name off those
> computers?

He leans in closer as Ann suffers.

DAN

I'm not doing it anymore... that's it. I just
want my appeal date for Employment and
Support...

ANN

[Whispered] Please listen to me Dan... this is
a huge decision... it could be weeks till your
appeal comes through... there is no time limit
for a mandatory reconsideration...

DAN

I have a time limit.

ANN

And you might not win... [glancing around
her again] keep signing on, get someone to
help with the online job searches... if not you
might lose everything... [Looking round her,
quietly]... I've seen it before... good people,
honest people, on the street...

Dan holds her eye for a few moments.

DAN

[Quietly] Thank you Ann. If you lose your
self-respect... you're done for.

He gets up and leaves her still holding his Claimant Commitment
Form.

Dan walks out and winks at the security guard.

DAN

See you sooner than you think...

It leaves him confused.

## 38. OUTSIDE THE JOBCENTRE (SAME DAY)

Dan turns left to a huge expanse of wall, part of the Jobcentre, and it is clearly visible from the busy street. He stops and takes out something from his pocket. He shakes it, and then starts writing in big black letters from a spray can.

Several passers-by stop in amazement, stunned to see an older man with a spray can.

He writes... 'I, Daniel Blake... N. I. No. WL 75 11 67D...'

INSIDE: The security guard runs towards the office of the manager.

Dan continues spraying outside.

'...Demand my appeal date before I starve...'

The manager and guard rush to Dan.

> SECURITY GUARD
> What the fuck are you playing at?

Dan shakes the can while he holds their eye.

> MANAGER
> Call the police.

Dan turns to the wall again. The two officials stare at the words being spelled out as the security guard tries to get through to the police. More people gather around and some take photos on their mobiles.

'And... change... shite... music... on... your... phones.'

He hesitates for a second before adding a big exclamation mark.

Laughter and a cheer from some youngsters.

### DAN

[To the manager] New hobby... Do you think
I should put this on my CV?

He moves closer to the security guard who is now talking to
the police.

### DAN

And tell them I'm going to do this every
single day till I get my appeal date.

Dan walks back to the wall, and sits on the ground under the
writing. A small gathering has crowded round. Several shout
encouragement, others laugh and insult the officials. A really
crazy looking man appears, a bit over the equator on some
cocktail, stumbles over and starts mouthing the words on the
wall to himself. On finishing (some time) he pulls off his jumper
and shirt to reveal a chest heavily tattooed.

### CRAZY MAN

[Still looking at the wall, fist in air] Yes!!!!!
Words of wisdom! [To Dan] You are 'the
man', wee man.

Another youngster comes over to Dan with a mobile and a
selfie stick.

### YOUTH

Can I have a selfie bud?

A police car pulls up and the officers run over to the action. The
two policemen arrest Dan and attempt to bring him over to the
vehicle. But they are being harassed by the bare-chested crazy
man much to everyone's amusement.

CRAZY MAN

Brothers… you're arresting an innocent man!

POLICEMAN 1

Clear off, or you'll be coming too…

CRAZY MAN

A miscarriage of injustice!

POLICEMAN 2

Shut it you if you know what's good for you!

CRAZY MAN

Should be arresting the wankers who thought
up sanctions! That preachy baldy cunt… Ian
Duncan what's his face! Him with the piles…

POLICEMAN 2

Beat it, clear off!

CRAZY MAN

And the posh dicks in mansions who came up
with the bedroom tax for disabled, including
my fucking one-legged granny…

He starts hopping around on one leg just out of range.

POLICEMAN 1

Your last warning!

CRAZY MAN

Not much fun… [still hopping like crazy]…
a pensioner on one leg… how many spare
bedrooms does that Chancellor of the Fucking
Extractor got?… Georgie Chops… schoolboy
fart…

POLICEMAN 2

I want you out of here now!

CRAZY MAN

Him and his Bullingdon Club Toss Pots!
Sun shining out their arse! Posh Eton twats
trashing lives! [Pounding the windscreen to
the police van] Fucking windbags! Keep your
greasy hands off The People's Bedrooms,
outlaw sanctions... justice for one-legged
grannies!

POLICEMAN 2

I said clear off!

CRAZY MAN

This man is a hero... [Pointing at graffiti] Sir
Daniel Blake!... Should be a statue made...
a fucking scholar! [Doing so] I salute you! A
martyr, a prophet in your own lifetime!

Dan salutes him back from the van, as the crazy man stands to
attention, bare-chested, on one leg (left leg held up by his left
hand) as he salutes with his right as the van moves off.

## 39. POLICE STATION (SAME DAY)

Dan looks spent as he faces a senior officer at the counter who
finishes off paperwork.

OFFICER

Okay Mr Blake... we're nearly there...
checked out your address...

DAN

What happens now?

OFFICER

...You are likely to get a summons for
Criminal Damage and possibly one for a
Public Order offence too... all depends...
[looking up at him]... graffiti... at your age,
on a public building... think you would be
ashamed of yourself...

OUTSIDE: As Dan walks down the steps he passes a police car.
Two officers stand by it, one on the phone, the other recognises
Dan.

POLICEMAN

Dan! You remember me?... You worked with
my old man...

DAN

Robbie's son... say hello to him for me...

POLICEMAN

Will do... [checking around him]... what are
you doing here?

DAN

It's a long story... [remembering] Jimmy,
that's your name...

## 40. STREET OUTSIDE DAN'S FLAT (SAME DAY)

China and Piper are walking to their building when a police car
pulls to a halt swiftly beside them. Their faces turn pale.

They can't believe their eyes when Dan steps out and the police
car pulls off again. They are gobsmacked. Dan looks drained
too and moves towards them.

DAN

Post Office tipped them off... they are
closing in... police, customs, coast guards,
Interpol, Chinese Government... they know
everything about the trainers...


PIPER

Jesus Christ!


DAN

[To China] Even the shoe sizes... got your
emails... phone numbers...


CHINA

Fuck!


DAN

I never said a word... not a word... even
when the drips started on my forehead...
hands behind my back... Chinese torture...


CHINA

Dan you bastard!! Think I might have shat
myself! [Pulling at his trousers] Not joking...


PIPER

Fuck... good one Dan... pissed myself...


The boys laugh in relief.


PIPER

What are you doing with the police?


DAN

Fixing their windows...

                              CHINA
              We've hardly seen you... Are you okay Dan?


                               DAN
                Perfect. Never felt better.


They head towards the building, though China glances at Dan.

Fade.


## 41. DAN'S FLAT (3 WEEKS LATER)

Daisy walks up the stairs to Dan's flat. She carries a plastic
tupperware container carefully in her hand, not wanting to
upset the contents.

She moves along the external walkway towards Dan's door. She
knocks loudly and then peers through the letter box.


                              DAISY
              Dan... [louder] Dan! It's me, Daisy... I know
              you're in there... [No answer]... I counted the
              days... over a month... I'm not leaving till I
              see you...


Still no answer as she peers through.


                              DAISY
              [Long silence, then quietly] We know
              everything now... Mum spoke to your
              neighbour... told us lots of things...
              [Pause]... We didn't know about your heart
              Dan ... Why didn't you tell us? [Silence
              for a moment]... Going out at night... not
              answering the door... not answering our calls.
              Mum has been crying her heart out... why
              won't you speak to her? [Pause] No credit on
              the phone? That happened to us a lot...


                               122

She lays down the flap of the letter box, sits down, and leans up against the wall for several long moments.

She hears a creak inside. She opens up the letter box again.

> DAISY
> I heard the creak... you have no idea how
> stubborn I can be.

Long moment.

> DAISY
> It's cold out here... I'm freezing...

> DAN'S VOICE
> [Low energy] Please Daisy... I'm not feeling
> very well... I promise to come visit you...

> DAISY
> I can tell by your voice. You don't mean it, do
> you?

Silence.

> DAN
> Did your mum send you?

> DAISY
> She doesn't know I'm here. She's out at work
> and Dylan is with a friend. [Pause] I cooked
> you some couscous... the way Grannie taught
> me... I made it for you... and Dylan sent you
> his lollipop... he's really missing you too...

She takes it from her pocket and sticks it through the letter box. It bounces on the floor.

Still silence.

> DAISY
>
> Can I ask one question?

> DAN
>
> Okay.

> DAISY
>
> Did you help us?

> DAN
>
> Suppose so…

> DAISY
>
> So why can't I help you?

Silence.

> DAISY
>
> Is it because I'm a kid?

> DAN
>
> I felt ashamed… a bit lost Daisy.

> DAISY
>
> Do you think I don't know about that?

A moment, then door opens. Daisy is shocked at the sight. He has a white, scraggly beard, messed-up hair, stooped, dirty clothes and he is a bag of bones.

His face looks grey and emaciated. The carpet is gone. He grips on to the corner of the wall for support and can barely stand.

> DAISY
>
> Oh Dan… Dan! Dan!!!

She grips him in shock around the waist and bursts out crying, her face sinking into him. He grips her too as he nearly cracks as well.

> DAN
> I'm sorry Daisy… I'm fine.

> DAISY
> No! No!… You're not Dan!… You're not… I've lost enough friends…

He cups his hand round the back of her head.

> DAN
> Don't fret sweetheart…

Fade.

## 42. STREETS AND GOVERNMENT BUILDING (4 WEEKS LATER)

Dan and Katie, arms linked for support, walk through streets. They are at ease together.

They make their way over a walkway towards the city centre.

> DAN
> Never been the nervy sort Katie, but I'm nervous about this…

> KATIE
> Only natural Dan… means so much…

> DAN
> Waited so long… just want it over.

KATIE

You've got all your papers, well prepared...
someone to represent you... [squeezing his
arm] and you're coming round to ours tonight
to celebrate. Kids can't wait.

Dan smiles at the thought.

They eventually reach their destination and climb up the steps
of a nondescript building. Outside, several claimants smoke and
look anxious.

INSIDE: Dan and Katie face a receptionist who examines lists
in front of him. Dan holds his eye.

DAN

Daniel Blake... here for my appeal for
reinstatement of my right to Employment and
Support Allowance...

RECEPTIONIST

Thank you sir... your welfare rights officer is
inside waiting for you...

WAITING ROOM: Several applicants and their families wait
nervously for their appeal.

Dan and Katie stand and speak in one corner to an energetic
welfare rights officer who is flicking through his papers and
giving Dan an update.

Dan listens carefully and it's obvious he is anxious.

WELFARE OFFICER

The appeal is heard by a legally qualified
chairperson and a doctor...

Dan lets out a deep breath.

DAN

Fingers crossed... if I lose this one, I'll be on
the street...

WELFARE OFFICER

I got a fresh report from your doctor,
consultant, your physio too... they are
furious!... You are going to win this Dan... I
do this every week... I'll bet my life on it...

Katie pulls his arm tighter, linked round hers, lifted by his
optimism.

KATIE

Told you...

WELFARE OFFICER

And I'll get payment backdated for all these
months... just be yourself... answer the
questions... and relax... I'm really confident...

DAN

Need to get a few things off my chest... will
they listen to me?

WELFARE OFFICER

Least they can do...

The welfare rights officer catches sight of an official coming
out of the hearing room. He heads towards him and they talk.
Dan and Katie catch sight of the hearing room beyond them,
the table, the chairs, and three soberly dressed individuals who
will take the hearing. It raises the tension.

DAN

[Whispering to Katie] Funny... they have my
life in their hands... thanks for coming Katie.

She grips his arm tighter. Face to face.

> KATIE
> Thanks for asking... stubborn old bastard.

A moment between them. She gives him a peck on the cheek.

The officer holds up his hands to them indicating five minutes.

> DAN
> I'll have a quick freshen up... get my head
> together...

Dan heads towards the toilet.

TOILET: Dan stares at his face in the mirror for a moment or two. He splashes his face with water, once, twice... the bending down seems to have made him dizzy. He grips the sink. His face suddenly contorts, and he collapses with a terrible thud.

WAITING ROOM: A panic-stricken man comes running in.

> MAN
> Phone for an ambulance! A man's collapsed in
> the toilet! Anyone know first aid?

Pandemonium as several people rush to the toilet to help, including the official who runs the hearing.

> KATIE
> Is it an older man with a black suit?

> MAN
> That's him!

> KATIE
> Oh Dan!

She rushes into the toilet. The officer is already giving him first aid. He tries to restart his heart with a first aid manoeuvre which becomes increasingly desperate.

Katie is overcome and is on her knees beside him. She grips his hand.

> KATIE
> Come on Dan!... You can make it! Come on!

The officer keeps at it, pounding and then checking for breath.

> OFFICER
> Oh Christ... I think we've lost him.

> KATIE
> [Pulling his hand to her breast] Noooooooo! Dan!! Not now... you can't go now... it's not your time...

Fade.

## 43. CREMATORIUM (5 DAYS LATER)

The simplest and cheapest coffin possible sits up at the front. To the side, a vicar stands quietly in respect.

By a little table there is the photograph of Dan and his wife Molly that was on the wall in his home. Nearby, one of his most delicate mobiles hangs, and gently twirls. By the table, Katie, Daisy, and Dylan stand in respect, each holding a single red rose as they look out at the dozen or so mourners, including China and Piper, Joe and several mates from the sawmill, a few others faces not recognizable, and Ann, the Jobcentre coach, sits by herself at the back.

The undertaker nods at Katie who steps forward to say a few words. She has difficulty containing herself.

KATIE

They call this a pauper's funeral... the cheapest slot, 9 am. But Dan was no pauper to us... [looking over at her children] was he? He gave us what money cannot buy... [Holding up a single sheet of paper] I found this note on him when he died... [Looking down at it] He always wrote in pencil... he wanted to say this at his appeal, but never got the chance. [Pause] I will believe to my dying breath that this lovely man had a lot more to give, and that he was driven to an early grave by the State.

She takes a couple of deep, nervous breaths, and then reads.

KATIE

I am not a client, a customer, nor a service user... I am not a shirker, a scrounger, a beggar nor a thief... I am not a National Insurance number, nor a blip on screen... I paid my dues, never a penny short, and proud to do so. I don't tug the forelock but look my neighbour in the eye, and help him if I can. I don't accept or seek charity. My name is Daniel Blake, I am a man, not a dog. As such, I demand my rights. I demand you treat me with respect. I, Daniel Blake, am a citizen, nothing more, nothing less. Thank you.

Katie kisses the paper and then looks out at the mourners.

Fade to black.

# Ken Loach
*Director*

**There were rumours that *Jimmy's Hall* was going to be your last film. Was that ever the case, and if so what persuaded you to make *I, Daniel Blake?***

That was a rash thing to have said. There are so many stories to tell. So many characters to present...

**What lies at that root of the story?**

The universal story of people struggling to survive was the starting point. But then the characters and the situation have to be grounded in lived experience. If we look hard enough, we can all see the conscious cruelty at the heart of the State's provision for those in desperate need and the use of bureaucracy, the intentional inefficiency of bureaucracy, as a political weapon: 'This is what happens if you don't work; if you don't find work you will suffer.' The anger at that was the motive behind the film.

**Where did you start your research?**

I'd always wanted to do something in my home town, which is Nuneaton in the middle of the Midlands, and so Paul and I went and met people there. I'm a little involved with a charity called Doorway, which is run by a friend Carol Gallagher. She introduced Paul and me to a whole range of people who were unable to find work for various reasons – not enough jobs being the obvious one. Some were working for agencies on insecure wages and had nowhere to live. One was a very nice young lad who took us to his room in a shared house helped by Doorway and the room was Dickensian. There was a mattress on the floor, a fridge but pretty well nothing else. Paul asked him would it be rude to see what he'd got in the fridge. He said 'No' and he opened the door: there was nothing, there wasn't milk, there wasn't a biscuit, there wasn't anything. We asked him when was the last time he went without food, he said that the week before he'd been without food for four days. This is just straight hunger and he was desperate. He'd got a friend who was working for an agency. His friend had been told by the agency at five o'clock one morning to get to a warehouse at six o'clock. He had no transport, but he got there somehow, he was told to wait, and at quarter past six he was told, 'Well there's no work for you today.' He was sent back so he got no money. This constant humiliation and insecurity is something we refer to in the film.

**Out of all the material you gathered and the people you met, how did you settle on a narrative?**
That's probably the hardest decision to take because there are so many stories. We felt we'd done a lot about young people – *Sweet Sixteen* was one – and we saw the plight of older people and thought that it often goes unremarked. There's a generation of people who were skilled manual workers who are now reaching the end of their working lives. They have health problems and they won't work again because they're not nimble enough to duck and dive between agency jobs, a bit of this and a bit of that. They are used to a more traditional structure for work and so they are just lost. They can't deal with the technology and they have health problems anyway. Then they are confronted by assessments for Employment and Support Allowance where you can be deemed fit for work when you're not. The whole bureaucratic, impenetrable structure defeats people. We heard so many stories about that. Paul wrote the character Daniel Blake and the project was under way.

**And your argument is that the bureaucratic structure is impenetrable by design...**

Yes. The Jobcentres now are not about helping people, they're about setting obstacles in people's way. There's a job coach, as they're called, who is now not allowed to tell people about the jobs available, whereas before they would help them to find work. There are expectations of the number of people who will be sanctioned. If the interviewers don't sanction enough people they themselves are put on 'Personal Improvement Plans'. Orwellian, isn't it? This all comes from research drawn from people who have worked at the DWP, they've worked in Jobcentres and have been active in the Trade Union, PCS – the evidence is there in abundance. With the sanctioning regime it means people won't be able to live on the money they've got and therefore foodbanks have come into existence. And this is something the government seems quite content about – that there should be foodbanks. Now they're even talking about putting job coaches into foodbanks, so the foodbanks are becoming absorbed in to the State as part of the mechanism of dealing with poverty. What kind of world have we created here?

**Do you feel it's a story that speaks mainly to these times?**

I think it has wider implications. It goes back to the Poor Law, the idea of the deserving and the undeserving poor. The working class have to be driven to work by fear of poverty. The rich have to be bribed by ever greater rewards. The political establishment have consciously used hunger and poverty to drive people to accept the lowest wage and most insecure work out of desperation. The poor have to be made to accept the blame for their poverty. We see this throughout Europe and beyond.

**What was it like going to film in foodbanks?**

We went to a number of foodbanks together and Paul went to more on his own. The story of what we show in the foodbank in the film was based on an incident that was described to Paul. Oh, foodbanks are awful; you see people in desperation. We were at a foodbank in Glasgow and a man came to the door. He looked in and he hovered and then he walked away. One of the women working there went after him, because he was obviously in need, but he couldn't face the humiliation of coming in and asking for food. I think that goes on all the time.

**Why did you decide to set the film in Newcastle?**
We went to a number of places – we went to Nuneaton, Nottingham, Stoke and Newcastle. We knew the North-West well having worked in Liverpool and Manchester so we thought we should try somewhere else. We didn't want to be in London because that has got huge problems but they're different and it's good to look beyond the capital. Newcastle is culturally very rich. It's like Liverpool, Glasgow, big cities on the coast. They are great visually, cinematic, the culture is very expressive and the language is very strong. There's a great sense of resistance; generations of struggle have developed a strong political consciousness.

**Describe the character of Daniel – who is he and what is his predicament?**
Dan is a man who's served his time as a joiner, a skilled craftsman. He's worked on building sites, he's worked for small builders, he's been a jobbing carpenter and still works with wood for his own enjoyment. But his wife has died, he's had a serious heart attack and nearly fell off some scaffolding; he's instructed not to work and he's still in rehabilitation, so he's getting Employment and Support Allowance. The film tells a story of how he tries to survive in that condition once he's been found 'fit to work'. He's resilient, good-humoured and used to guarding his privacy.

**And who is Katie?**

Katie is a single mother with two small children. She's been in a hostel in London when the local authority finds her a flat in the North where the rent will be covered by her housing benefit – that means the local authority doesn't have to make up the difference. The flat's fine, though it needs work, but then she falls foul of the system and she's immediately in trouble – she's got no family round her, no support, no money. Katie is a realist. She comes to recognise that her first responsibility is to survive somehow.

**Much of the story deals with suffocating bureaucracy. How did you make that dramatic?**

What I hope carries the story is that the concept is familiar to most of us. It's the frustration and the black comedy of trying to deal with a bureaucracy that is so palpably stupid, so palpably set to drive you mad. I think if you can tell that truthfully and you're reading the subtext in the relationship between the people across a desk or over a phone line, that should reveal the comedy of it, the cruelty of it – and, in the end, the tragedy of it. 'The poor are to blame for their poverty' – this protects the power of the ruling class.

**What were you looking for in your Dan and in your Katie when you cast Dave Johns and Hayley Squires?**

Well, for Dan we looked for the common sense of the common man. Every day he's turned up for work, he's worked alongside mates; there's the crack of that, the jokes, the way you get through the day; that's been his life until he was sick and until his wife needed support. And so alongside the sense of humour you want someone quite sensitive and nuanced.

And for Katie, again it's someone driven by circumstance who is realistic but has potential; she's been trying to study, she failed at school but she's been studying with the Open University. We looked for someone with sensitivity but also gutsy courage. And, as with Dan, absolute authenticity.

**Dave Johns is a stand-up comic as well as an actor. Why did you cast him as Dan?**

The traditional stand-up comedian is a man or woman rooted in working-class experience, and the comedy comes out of that experience. It often comes out of hardship, joking about the comedy of survival. But the thing with comedians is they've got to have good timing – their timing is absolutely implicit in who they are. And they usually have a voice that comes from somewhere and a persona which comes from somewhere, so that's what we were looking for. Dave's got that. Dave's from Byker, which is where we filmed some of the scenes, he's a Geordie, he's the right age, and he's a working-class man who makes you smile, which is what we wanted.

**How did you come to cast Hayley Squires as Katie?**

We met a lot of women who were all interesting in different ways but again, Hayley's a woman with a working-class background and she was just brilliant. Every time we tried something out she was dead right. She doesn't soften who she is or what she says in any way, she's just true really, through and through.

**How was the shoot?**

To begin with, Paul's writing is always very precise, as well as being full of life. This means we rarely shoot material we don't use. The critical thing in filming is planning. It is preparation; working things out; getting everyone cast before you start; getting all the locations in place before you start. To do all that you need a crew, a group of people who absolutely understand the project and are creatively committed to it. And all those things we had: amazing efficiency from everyone and great humour. That's what gets you through, because it means all your effort is then productive. Working with good friends is a delight and, crucially, we even got a little coffee machine that used to follow us around. That was a key element: a good espresso got us all through the day.

**You changed how you edited this film from previous ones. How and why?**

We'd been cutting on film for many years but we found that the infrastructure for cutting on film was just disappearing. The biggest problem was the cost of printing the sound rushes on mag stock and also printing all the film rushes. It was more than I could justify so, reluctantly, we cut on Avid. It has some advantages but I found cutting on film was a more human way of working – you can see what you've done at the end of the day. Avid seems quicker but I don't think the overall time taken is any less. I just find the tactile quality of film is more interesting.

**Do you make films hoping to bring about change and, if so, what would that mean in the case of *I, Daniel Blake*?**

Well it's the old phrase isn't it: 'Agitate, Educate, Organise'. You can agitate with a film – you can't educate much, though you can ask questions – and you can't organise at all, but you can agitate. And I think to agitate is a great aim because being complacent about things that are intolerable is just not acceptable. Characters trapped in situations where the implicit conflict has to be played out, that is the essence of drama. And if you can find that drama in things that are not only universal but have a real relevance to what's going on in the world, then that's all the better. I think anger can be very constructive if it can be used; anger that leaves the audience with something unresolved in their mind, something to do, something challenging.

**It is the 50th anniversary of *Cathy Come Home* this year. What parallels are there between this new film and that film?**

They are both stories of people whose lives are seriously damaged by the economic situation they're in. It's been an idea we've returned to again and again but it's particularly sharp in *I, Daniel Blake*. The style of film-making, of course, is very different.

When we made *Cathy* we ran about with a hand-held camera, set up a scene, shot it and we were done. The film was shot in three weeks.

In this film the characters are explored more fully. Both Katie and Dan are seen in extremis. In the end, their natural cheerfulness and resilience are not enough. Certainly politically the world that this film shows is even more cruel than the world that Cathy was in. The market economy has led us inexorably to this disaster. It could not do otherwise. It generates a working class that is vulnerable and easy to exploit. Those who struggle to survive face poverty. It's either the fault of the system or it's the fault of the people. They don't want to change the system, therefore they have to say it's the fault of the people.

Looking back, we should not be surprised at what has happened. The only question is – what do we do about it?

## Cast

*Dave Johns*
*Hayley Squires*

**Dave Johns**
*Dan*

**Who is Dan?**
Dan is in his late 50s and he's a guy who's worked all his life as a carpenter. He takes pride in his work and he makes these little carved fish in his spare time. He's an honest bloke, he's very straightforward; he's got a good sense of humour. He's very dignified and if he says, 'I'll do something,' he'll do it. He's been looking after his wife who had a mental illness but since she died he's a bit lost. Then he has the heart attack, a doctor tells him he can't work and he finds himself against this authority, these jobsworths, who won't budge. That's the thing that raises the hackles and he tries to deal with it in his own way by being quite frank, keeping his dignity, using his sense of humour. But he's finding it harder and harder because they've got everything stacked in their favour. The system's wearing him down.

Then he meets Katie who's come up from London with her two kids and they've become friends. She's up against it and I think he probably sees Katie as a cause. He wants to help, even to the point where at first he doesn't realise he's in a bad place himself.

**How did you come to be cast?**
Oh, God! Unbelievable! I'm a stand-up comic. I've done bits and bobs of acting in theatre mainly, and last year a producer I'd worked with said to me that he'd just had this actor's brief come in. He said it was improv, comic – right up my street.

So I just wrote an email to Kahleen [Crawford, Casting Director] and I said, 'I'm a stand-up comic, I've done a bit of acting. They said you're looking for somebody, I don't have any CV or anything, but here's my website.' And then a couple of weeks later I was called in to meet Ken. We had a bit of a chat about stuff I was doing, and we talked about my dad – he was a joiner in the North East, so I knew something about Dan and his world.

Then I did a casting, and the first person I did my improv with was Hayley [Squires] who went on to get the part. We did this scene, it worked great. Personally I was happy just to have met Ken – and then they called me back. Finally, after a few more times he phoned us: 'Hi, it's Ken,' he goes, 'Would you like to be in my film?' I'm going, 'Would I like to be in your film? Do you think I have to think about it, like?'

**How did you find filming?**
First day, to tell you the truth, I was shitting myself, I really was. There's a sad little voice in your head that goes, 'You're going to get caught here. You're going to get found out here, you cannot do this,' and I'm going, 'Go away,' you know.

But Ken was lovely: he said, 'Just think it.' It sounds so obvious, but suddenly it was like a door opened, you know. You're drawing on all sorts of experiences, like thinking about my dad, and his life and how he was. I mean, this might sound a bit arsy, but it's like it seeps in to you. You're not just going, 'Oh this bloke wrote these words and I just have to say them.' If you think it and you live it, it seems to go inside you, and it seems to come out natural and real. The minute I sussed out what he meant by that everything seemed to come into place.

I'd really like to thank Ken for going with me on this and making me something that I didn't know was in us. To be able to channel those emotions in a drama – I mean we did this one scene where it was just Katie talking to me in a room. I knew there was people around, but I never even twigged they were till I heard Ken go, 'Okay, end it there.' I was still crying in the corner, do you know what I mean?

## What did you learn about the benefits system from the story?

Well, I was amazed, 'cause, you know, the last time I signed on employment benefit was probably in the 70s when I left school. It was the Labour Exchange then. You went down and you said, 'I haven't got any work.' They'd go, 'Okay then, well you sign on. What sort of work are you looking for?' And then you went down and collected your money. I don't think people actually realise what they try to make people do now: it's all to get them off the system. I believe it's to sicken people. That's come as a shock to me. I think it's 50 years since *Cathy Come Home* this year. And nothing's changed.

## How did you prepare?

Well, I went on a woodworking course. There's a place down in Byker, underneath the bridge where people who are homeless or have problems can go and restore furniture. Then the furniture gets sold in the shop so it's self-funding. They've got a guy there who's a wood carver, so I went in for two days and learnt how to carve the fish that Dan likes to carve. I did one from scratch myself, you know, sanded it all up and gave it to my daughter. It meant I could handle the tools properly in the film and when we did the scenes of me woodcarving it looked authentic. And actually I found it quite therapeutic, to just, you know, sit there and sand a bit of wood. My daughter couldn't believe I'd made it myself. Neither could I, to be honest.

**Hayley Squires**
**Katie**

**Who is Katie?**

Katie is a 28-year-old woman from south London who has a daughter of eleven and a son of nine. She is very bright, wants to learn but two years prior to her moving to Newcastle she was a victim of a revenge eviction in London. She was renting a house from a private landlord, made a complaint that the boiler wasn't working and was chucked out, which is something that is rife in London at the moment. So she had to get out of her house and as a result of that was placed in a homeless hostel by the council. She ended up living there for two years, before the council got in touch and said, 'We can offer you a place – but it's in Newcastle.' She's got no choice – she has to move. But she's never been to Newcastle before. Mum's back in London, she's not very well, so she's got nobody up there.

When we first meet Katie the very first scene is her going into the Jobcentre for her transferral appointment, to register the new address and go over her Job Seeker's agreement. She ends up being half an hour late with the kids because they get lost – they don't know the city. And then she's told that she's going to be sanctioned. That then means she doesn't have any money for a month. So when you first meet her she's already done over.

**How does she meet Dan?**

He's at the Jobcentre for his own reason, he tries to help her, there's an argument and they get removed. From there they form a friendship with each other because they're in not dissimilar circumstances. I mean, he's a 59-year-old man who's fallen ill and he's trying to get back to work. He's lost his wife through illness and he's met with the bureaucracy of it all, you know, of not being able to use a computer or meeting the demands that you have to meet. At the beginning he looks out for Katie, helps her with the heating and the cooking and the kids. Katie ends up in a situation where Dan takes her and the kids to a foodbank. She hasn't eaten for a few days; things get pretty drastic there.

**What is your background and how did you come to be cast?**
I graduated in 2010 from Rose Bruford College. I did a degree in acting. I write as well as act, and I've just started on a screenplay. I had a very quiet first two years coming out of drama school and then things picked up and I've done bits of TV and supporting roles in films. I'd done a couple of tapes for Kahleen, the casting director, but I'd never met her in person. I got a call in the summer, last year, to say Ken Loach's new film's casting and he's just meeting women and girls from London that fit this age group. Don't know what the project's about, there's no script, there's no sides, he just wants you to go in and have a chat. So I met Ken and Kahleen and we talked for about 15 minutes. It all went from there.

**What did they ask you about?**
They asked me about my life, where I grew up, what my parents were like, what they did for a living. I grew up in south London and then when I was 14 we moved to Kent. They wanted to get out of London. So I spoke to Ken about the transition of being in London and moving to a small town. We talked about what I would be doing if I wasn't acting, my brother, my family. If I hadn't got on well at school then I don't think my situation would be too far away from Katie's.

Friends of mine are in a similar position, not to the point of sanctions and all the rest of it but on their own with children. I've grown up surrounded by it.

**How did you find Dave Johns when you first met him?**
It was so nice because we just talked. I'm not saying all actors are vain but a man in his sixties who's been in the game for however many years, you're used to going and doing audition after audition and presenting a version of yourself each time you go in. Whereas with Dave, he was cracking jokes while we were in the room so that made it very relaxed and very calm. It didn't feel like he was trying to show what he could do – it felt like we could just talk to each other and anything that they needed to see was going to come out of that.

**Was this film different to others you've worked on?**
Yeah it was completely different. I mean I do very little theatre. I trained in theatre but I've only done one play since I left drama school; everything else has been screen. Normally you get your sides, get your character breakdown, if you're lucky you get the full script to have a proper read. And of course with Ken you don't. One thing I picked up was he very rarely used the word 'improvisation'; he said 'conversations' instead. Then he would go, 'This is what the situation is, this is where you've been, this is where you'd like to get to and now just talk to each other.' And it was lovely.

Overall it's been the best experience I've ever had – it makes me a bit emotional thinking about it! Ken is a hero of mine, having watched his films and knowing what he's all about and what he represents. Same with Paul and Rebecca – the work they've done over the last 20-odd years is amazing. It's been unlike anything I've ever done before, what with not knowing what's coming and placing a lot of trust in your director and also your crew. But it's great to be able to tell that story and be that character. And it hasn't been like being part of a cast... it's been like being part of a crew. There's a calmness and a support you get from everyone who's involved. It's like a safe circle that they're all on the outside of and you get to be in the middle.

## Production

*Rebecca O'Brien*
*Robbie Ryan*
*Kahleen Crawford*
*Linda Wilson*
*Ray Beckett*
*Jonathan Morris*

### Rebecca O'Brien
*Producer*

#### How did this film come about?

I think basically both Paul and Ken were getting itchy feet. Paul
had been doing research into this area and encouraging Ken
to get involved. As usual, Paul came up with some interesting
stories and it became irresistible. Then Ken and Paul went and
looked at a few places; they went to a foodbank in Glasgow
and they went to various places in the Midlands, they went to
Stoke, they went to Nuneaton where Ken grew up and places
like that too. In part it was to see where might be good to shoot
but also to explore the extent of the stories and meet people that
Paul had contacted. That was in the winter and then Paul went
away and I don't think he started writing until March or April
[2015] actually, even May, and then very soon there was a script.
I was doing another film but as soon as that finished, we made a
decision that it would be worth doing this, and quickly. I think
we all just felt that it's so current and so vital to tell these stories
that we decided to go for it and just do it while it's completely
relevant and hot.

#### What is the film about?

It's about the struggle to survive, a story that returns again and
again in different times and circumstances.

**Were you concerned that such a story might lack inherent drama?**

Not at all. Paul Laverty's outrage and his constant flow of research allows him to find the stories that are worth telling. And then his ability to build a framework to hang the stories on is so good that he makes it seem effortless.

**How was *I, Daniel Blake* funded?**

Well, as ever our wonderful French partners are on board. Why Not Productions and Wild Bunch sales company cash-flowed us throughout pre-production and preparation. We decided to go very quickly, in July in the end, so I put my application in to BFI and also the BBC in June, and I sent them a script as soon as I got it. That's a very quick turnaround for them but BBC Films came on board – the first time we've had BBC Films equity - and the BFI did as well. Because it was so quick, I think they'd spent a lot of their money this year so we didn't get maybe as much as we normally might but our French partners were brilliant in helping to fill the gap. They also brought Les Films du Fleuve, our Belgian partners, on board again and we did a co-production with Belgium as well as France. Overall it's a slightly lower budget film than some of our recent ones because it's a much smaller cast – it's more of a chamber piece really.

**Why did you choose to shoot in Newcastle?**

We chose Newcastle because it's a very defined city. We wanted something that said proper urban centre and also it's very beautiful. I suppose you want to demonstrate that these stories happen to people in great cities and in good parts of the country, and not just in places that are obviously down at heel. In Newcastle, there's a real cross section of people and places. It's also got a very dramatic look to it with its hills and the gorge of the river and all the bridges. There's something very strong about it as a place. I've always wanted to film there myself and I think Ken has too.

**What was the thinking behind bringing Katie up from London as a parallel to Dan's story?**

Dan's story might have seemed a bit bleak and thin by itself and I think you want to show that there are people who will support each other – there is kindness out there. Katie's story works very well because it's a counterpoint to what Dan is up against. Katie is struggling but in a different way. It would have been too linear if it was just Dan.

**It was suggested that *Jimmy's Hall* might be Ken's last narrative feature, but here he is back on fighting form. Do you feel like he has been re-energised by the subject matter?**

Yes. It's fantastic for both him and Paul to be doing something that is so immediately political and so important. It's absolutely current and there's something vital about making it. That vitality feeds into Ken and Paul and it shows itself in the film. It's still tough for anybody to make a film but the subject matter and working with the actors telling the story absolutely inspires Ken. I think it's fantastic seeing him so energised. On some days I think, 'God, if we could keep doing this forever…'

**Does political film-making even exist in Britain at the moment or are you ploughing a lone furrow?**

I'm sure there are some people who are concerned, but people shy away from politics so much. They think it's the kiss of death but I think with the younger generation becoming increasingly politicised, as the Corbyn vote indicated, there is a new interest. There are some political statements made by directors and even more so by artists, but I don't see a lot of political stories out there. You would think there would be more and yet Ken remains the spokesperson for all ages and has a lot of young fans. If you look at our social media, we're well followed: I think that's partly because there are very few people who will put their heads above the parapet and are not afraid of being overtly political.

Being older helps you: you've got nothing to lose so you can say what you think.

**Cathy Come Home came out 50 years ago in November. Do you see this film as a bookend?**

There are very powerful parallels. I do see this film very much as a bookend to what happened 50 years ago but it's a different story. I think this film demonstrates that there is no safety net for vulnerable people now, just as there was no safety net then. Now they have created jargon to neutralise the plight of desperate people. People are described as 'benefit units', you have to prove 'conditionality'. It's absurd. But there are many parallels with the past and I think it makes a big point that Ken is making a film about these issues 50 years on from that powerful moment. I think it just says that we need to keep making them.

**Robbie Ryan**
*Director of Photography*

### What were your first thoughts on the script?

I liked it. It was the whole runaround of bureaucracy coming through it that was the thing that struck me the most. The fact that Dan was up against just a ridiculous, backwards system that was never going to change for him, and it's getting worse. So that kind of 'Brazil' element got me in. I still can't quite get my head around the fact that that's actually a system that works here in England. Or doesn't work.

### How does a DOP read a script?

First of all I read it for the story and what I could bring to the story; and then second, in normal circumstances I'd read it from a technical aspect. But with Ken's films you don't really do that because you read it knowing that it'll be done in a 'Ken' style. Really you're trying to figure out how he would do it. In a way, I try and see how Ken is going to approach the film and not how I would approach the film. That's kind of the way that the Team Loach thing works, and I like that – I enjoy dropping into a film like that because you know you are in safe hands with Ken. A lot of the time you go into a film and a script not knowing if the director has the vision that you have – and you have to get to know each other a bit. But after several films working with Ken, I know now what he likes and what he doesn't, and so I see the script in that way.

**Does that compromise your ability to innovate?**

No. I love naturalism in film anyway. I like seeing stuff in front of the camera that feels honest and real, and that means you don't bring a lot to it – what's in front of the camera is the thing that's important. Ken's films are more about faces and people than they are about places. The place obviously is an important part of it but it's about the people's lives within that space, so in a way I always like knowing that we are going to be filming interesting people in interesting situations. From a creative point of view, it's much more about trying to get it to feel real in this style of Ken's. You know he doesn't like lights very often so you have to try and keep that to a minimum. The idea is to not bring in too many of the trappings of film-making in to the way you film it.

**What sort of look were you and Ken aiming for in this film?**

Well actually this one was interesting because I found out something new about Ken this time! For a while he was going to make the film in black and white. He showed us all *Looks and Smiles*, a film of his that he shot in 1981. I had never seen it. Chris Menges shot it and it's really an amazing looking film because the black and white lends itself to a lot of dark, silhouetted foregrounds. It was shot in many similar settings to *I, Daniel Blake* – lots of dull queues and offices - but because it was 1981 everything looked a lot more Victorian almost. There are these beautiful big windows with daylight coming in and a lot of silhouettes and people. We looked at that as a kind of reference, and it was interesting that Ken was going back to an old film to refer to. In the end he decided not to go black and white because it may have given the wrong message and it lacked the honesty and brutality of what he was trying to do. But we kept in mind the whole idea of trying to keep something with a little bit of a silhouette in the foreground.

**How did that work in the stark light of a modern Jobcentre?**

That Jobcentre was a little bit tricky because it was quite bright with that flat, fluorescent light. But it did have its own look and I think Ken was keen on that being a green and aggressive space. He didn't want it to feel like a nice place. From a photographic point of view, it was about going with whatever was in the place we were filming and trying to make the most of it.

**How did you shoot the scene when Dan spray paints his name on the wall outside?**

That was a long day. We had two cameras and we shot it a lot of times. Newcastle was actually really pleasant for the whole shoot but that one day, the weather was coming in and that road was like a wind channel. With that being a set piece as such, we had repeats of the graffiti stuff. The aim was to get all the coverage and make it all feel like it was happening at the right time. We knew where the sun was going to be and we kept it pretty consistent. In a way, filming with Ken is all about trying to keep the consistency of things. You are out in the elements, sometimes the sun can come out or go in and it's about just running with it.

**Were there any technical adjustments to Ken's process?**

Normally Ken has got a system that is not for breaking. It's the way he has done it for the last 25 years, and it's a joy to watch him because he knows what works and what tells the story best. He'll be shooting things on one lens and then he'll realise that the next lens that we'd be shooting on was a bit wider than the first one so we'd go back to do the first one again on a wider lens so that the progression of the scene wouldn't jump different lens sizes, like from tight to wide to tight... you only begin to see these things when you have done a few films with him; you see the mindset of how he is doing it. It's meticulous.

This time he did do something different though – and I was

shocked! He says, 'What's that thing where you attach something to you and you move with the camera? They walk around with it; it looks like a vest or something.' He was talking about a Steadicam. That was the shot he wanted. Everybody looked at each other shocked, because this had just come out of the blue. It's the bit in the film where they are all outside the foodbank and he wanted to get the movements across all these faces that were all looking to get fed. He thought that was the best way he could do it – I think it was the first time Ken had ever done a Steadicam. The old dog with new tricks all of a sudden. The thing is with Ken is that he knows that doing things differently just for the sake of it can mean you lose focus. That's the sign of a good director: he knows the way he can best get across what he wants to say.

## Kahleen Crawford
*Casting Director*

### Describe the casting process for *I, Daniel Blake*

We get the script and we always start with geography on Ken's films. Almost the first question I ever ask Ken is to draw a map to show what area I can get people from and we agreed it had to be Newcastle or Sunderland or even places like Hartlepool. But we fairly quickly narrowed it down quite a lot – we wanted it to be a Geordie. Then I went to actors' agents and looked at actors. There weren't lots in the right age group, but there were some that were fantastic – yet maybe too well known. Ken just wanted it to be really simple, something the audience would just watch and not be cluttered with preconceptions of a well-known, local actor. Once we'd done a lot of the actors, we also looked at the comedy clubs and at singers and musicians.

### You quite often look to comedians. Why?

I just think Ken over the years has had so much success doing that, even sometimes just in smaller parts. They're people who know how to present themselves and to perform to an audience and they're just really rooted. Dave Johns actually heard about it through a friend and so he wrote us an email.

### What were you looking for in your Dan?

It's partly intuitive but Ken was saying that the things that were important to him were just a real, good, working man; the type of person that the story is about. He wanted it to be someone really grounded and local and just to have the voice. I mean, there are so many different versions of a Geordie accent. It's like in Glasgow there are so many different Glaswegians. Dave falls somewhere in the middle but he's very recognisably Geordie. He also feels like someone who could build things, things like furniture. Also, it's not maybe something that we made too explicit but I think that Dave just kind of gets the politics of it all. He comes from a certain background, he understands why this is unfair and he understands why the system shouldn't be like this. He remembers what the system used to be like and the values that there used to be that we've lost.

## Do you ever know it's the right person the instant they walk in the room?

You do sometimes – but then sometimes you're proven wrong. We like to have a chat, you come back, you try some stuff out, then you re-jig the chemistry and you try them out opposite different people. What is really exciting is seeing the process unfolding and seeing those people unfolding. Give them another scenario and something entirely different would come out of them. Here, a huge part of it for me was the chemistry between Dave and Hayley. There was something quite special there. They brought out the best in each other.

## What were you looking for in their characters' relationship?

I think it was really important to us that it wasn't a romance. I think that there are energies that you pick up from people when you know that they're a bit 'flirty Gerty from number 30' as we say in the office. There was nothing like that here – it was just a really nice, natural energy between them.

## Why is Hayley Squires right for Katie?

Hayley is really interesting, a really special talent. We took to her quite quickly and she's just mega smart. She's got the right voice that Ken wanted to hear – something really recognisably London. We need to know that she's very far away from home. Hayley's also got a lovely warmth but she's got a real fighting spirit and I think that you need that for Katie. You need to stick with Katie – she's not a victim because she's 'a victim' – she's genuinely a victim of circumstances. Hayley was a real well of ideas in the improvisation auditions and she gets rhythm and all that stuff because she's a writer. Hopefully she does justice to Paul's dialogue.

**Linda Wilson**
*Production Designer*

**Tell us about your previous work with Ken Loach**
The first film I ever did with Ken was *Ladybird, Ladybird*, 23 years ago. I did prop buying on that, working with Martin Johnson who was his original designer. I was very well trained up. Then I did *Land and Freedom* which was fantastic. Best working experience ever. And then I did *It's a Free World* eight or nine years ago. By then Martin had died and Fergus Clegg, who'd been art directing, had taken over. They contacted me about this film earlier in the year, because Fergus couldn't do it. I couldn't wait. They're always my favourite films to do because Ken's very charming, and incredibly focussed and knows what he wants. It's a process of delivering that with your own ideas that don't go too large.

**What were the challenges designing *I, Daniel Blake*?**
It's quite difficult for Ken. He has a very specific way of working and he likes everything to be nicely aged and look very normal and ordinary. It's actually quite hard for an art department to do that. Harder than a period drama actually, but somehow more rewarding. For the last few years I've set decorated on *Downton Abbey*, which was fantastic to do in beautiful places with chandeliers and whatever. But actually, it's much more interesting going round charity shops and looking for the perfect chair for the character in a film like this – and finding it. There's something about the way that Ken works. You're kind of putting

together the set in the way that the character would. So on this, the character of Dan would've bought his furniture several years ago from various places. We try to do it the same way and try to keep the palette all in the mid-tones. Nothing too bright. Nothing too new. It's a process of layering it so that it looks very realistic and nothing jumps out at you.

**What is layering?**
Layering is when you have, say, a texture on the wall. So you put a wallpaper with a texture and then you're painting it, and then you're aging it. And then you put a mirror or a picture. There'd be a lamp, then there'd be a bit more aging. Then there'll be some photographs, some in frames and then some just tucked in behind things. It's just starting with an empty wall and then bringing it to life, using only things that are right for the character.

**Can you say a bit about what Dan is like, in so far as it affects what his flat would be like?**
Right at the beginning we decided that he was quite a tidy man and quite proud. He'd looked after his wife, who'd died, so he'd had this whole backstory that we could reference if we wanted. Joss [Barratt, photographer] took pictures of him and his wife, Molly, as soon as she was cast. They went and did a photoshoot at Whitley Bay, and we framed all those and had them so they're all round the flat as a kind of added detail. We mended all the floorboards so they didn't creak, and sanded them and got them all to the right colour. We wanted to keep all the colours as a mid-tone, and make sure that everything like the records, the chairs, everything, was from the time when he got married and moved in to the flat. But then, obviously, the main part of the story is that he carves things, those wooden fish, so we had to put in all of his tools. All of our fish were carved at a Social Enterprise scheme called Under the Bridge. That was quite a difficult process, saying to people, 'Yes, like that but a bit longer

and a bit thinner, and a bit...' But they all got into it. They used to dread it when I went round for my fish checking. Ken came and had a look as well and met them. We decided it would be good if Dave went and had some lessons so that he knew how to do the carving. So he went and did that, and produced a fish and was very proud of it.

### How about Katie's flat?

What happens is that everyone has an idea of how something *might* look and we do a lot of research to find out how it would *actually* look. The storyline is she has moved to Newcastle from London and been put in accommodation, so we found the minimum that a landlord would have to provide. There's not very much in her flat, which is actually harder to do than full rooms. Just a sofa, a chair, a table and a couple of lamps. It is quite shocking actually. Hayley came round and saw it with the two actors who play her children. The little boy said, 'Uh, I wouldn't want to live here.' That was how we knew we'd got it right.

### Was the scene in the foodbank filmed at an actual foodbank?

We did it in a church hall where they do have a foodbank, but we brought in shelving and we got all of our food and donated it to them afterwards. It felt like a good kind of gesture to be able to make. I think that affected all of us quite a lot, because it's quite an extraordinary thing to see and to know it's going on.

### What about the Jobcentre set?

Jobcentres don't look like what people think they look like and they're quite hard to get in to if you're not signing on! They don't want you to come in and have a look, so it took quite a while for us to even get some reference points. As a set, we've made it very grey and monochrome. Lifeless I suppose. The life comes in the hostility of the actors playing security guards and managers.

**How did you design Dan's climactic graffiti scene?**
The 'wall' on which he sprays his name was built out of wood, in sections, and painted, then attached to the building society wall where we were filming. We had enough for three repeats and Dave did a trial run beforehand. We timed him doing it – originally it had his National Insurance number in as well, but that was just too much and quite a hard thing to learn in your head so Ken decided to take that out. It's a classic example of how a lot of organisation and time can go in to something, purely so that the audience won't notice it.

**Ray Beckett**
*Recordist*

**You've worked on sixteen films with Ken Loach but you've also won an Oscar for your Hollywood work. What keeps you coming back?**
The reason I come back is it's the way of film-making that challenges me the most. Ken offers all of his crew a unique challenge in their own departments to just get it right in what are actually quite difficult circumstances some times. On most films you do a lot in a studio where you can float walls and you've got a lot of control. But Ken will not do that. If the scene is in a house, he wants to film in an actual house. I'll often find myself stuck behind a fridge or something, then having to move between takes, but you have to find a way, technically: there's no possibility of doing ADR [recording dialogue in a studio at a later date] – that's out of the question. Ken will do everything he can to make the environment quiet enough to make that happen. He wouldn't normally, for example, record near an airport. But if he does we have to equip the actors so that we can hear them – and we can also hear the airport with good fidelity. The trick is if you've got that background noise, and you can't get rid of it, at least record it well. I use ambient mics to get the dialogue but also to have the background that the dialogue can sit in. The reason I love working with Ken is these technical challenges he throws at us every day. I would say that *I, Daniel Blake* wasn't as difficult as *Jimmy's Hall* – that film had lots of live music to be recorded. That was a serious

challenge that I really enjoyed; we were working in an Easy-Up in a force nine gale.

**What were the specific challenges on *I, Daniel Blake*?**
This script has got lots of phone calls in it, lots of people phoning in or phoning out. Ken always wants the actor holding the phone to hear the real voice of the actual person he's supposed to be listening to. And also, when he gets in to the cutting room, he wants to hear the effect as if it's coming through a phone. So we have contrived a system for mobile phones that seems to work pretty well: say we've got an actor in the street on their mobile and we want to hear who's on the other end? Well, the person at the other end making the call has a mobile in their left hand that's dialling the mobile you see on screen. At the same time they've got another mobile which goes through to my iPhone which is plugged in to one of the tracks on my mixer – so that Ken can hear. The problem with mobiles is you've got unpredictable delays, which we have to reconcile later on. But at least Ken gets what he wants, which is the real sound.

Another difficulty in the script we had to overcome is an incoming Skype call from China. Ken has this artifice that he wants the actors to really think that this guy on the computer *is* in China. (Only afterwards do the actors get told that he's down the corridor in the production office.) The thing with that was we wanted to get the sound as if it was coming from Skype. But the problem with Skype is sometimes it's a little bit garbled and difficult to understand. So I try and get a clean mix as well: another recordist recorded the actor live through a mic so that if the Skype line went down they always had that to go back to. But the best way to do it was to record the Skype call coming out of the speaker – and actually it worked fine.

**How did you get the never-ending hold music from the DWP helpline?**
The lawyer had to check that it was legal for us to dial in to the

DWP and record whatever was on their system and then I spent a morning on my iPhone dialling the DWP line recording it. The first time I dialled it was so early I nearly got through! But later on when it got busy I got in to this Vivaldi hell. I got a long track of 'press button one... press button four'. The most iniquitous thing is, you're paying for that – that's a premium line. It's not free. They're making money from homeless people on hold! And the Vivaldi hold music is synthesised – it's not even an orchestra.

**What's the significance of the 'Sailing By' theme for Dan and how did you get hold of it?**
There's a lovely scene where Dan is alone in his flat, whittling his fish, and then he hears 'Sailing By' on the radio. It's a very calm, contemplative moment. I think it sets up Dan as the character he really is, before this maelstrom hits him. He's a gentle craftsman, basically. Production got permission from the BBC to use 'Sailing By' and the late *Shipping Forecast* that immediately follows it, before the World Service comes on at one o' clock. I still have the music in my head.

**Jonathan Morris**
*Editor*

**What were your thoughts when you first saw the script?**
I thought it was a very interesting script. Quite a challenge I think for Ken to make it visual because it's quite wordy and several of the scenes are 'man on a phone' – not terribly exciting you might think. But of course that's where Ken works his magic.

**What are you looking for as an editor when you read a script?**
I'm looking for how difficult the scenes might be to cut. Music scenes in particular are always quite difficult to cut because the way Ken shoots them there's no playback or anything, people are doing it live and it's always quite a challenge to edit. But there was nothing like that here. In general I try not to read it too well, if that makes sense, because basically what I have in the end is not the script but only what Ken's shot.

**Do you have a role during shooting?**
When they're filming it's actually a stage of production which I dread because I'm very often the only person seeing rushes and if there's a problem or something which isn't quite as it should be I feel a little bit of pressure of do I tell Ken or does he know? Or if I tell them will that throw everyone into confusion? Do we need to reshoot this? Etc. etc. I mean it's not too bad quite frankly with Ken because he knows what he's doing.

**And then what happens after the shoot?**
Well this of course has been a very unusual film because we've cut it on Avid for the first time. This is a major thing really in that I've lost my pals in the cutting room, my assistant film editors either through retirement or the fact that they don't work on Avid.

It was shot on film and then put on to a drive and then ingested, I think is the word, into the computer. So no Steenbeck. I've had to train Ken really to work on the Avid and though we never row we've come close! Around about Friday afternoon every week Ken has pushed me a little bit: 'Why are you doing it that way? You never used to do it that way. What are you doing? Why are you doing that? What's going on?' Like most directors he is a control freak; unlike most directors he usually knows exactly what you're doing, but on the Avid he's not so sure. In my right fist there's a mouse, moving a little arrow around so he hasn't really liked that. But it's been absolutely brilliant and so much easier for me, I have to say.

**Why the change from editing film manually to on computer?**
For several reasons; the main one being that it's become harder and harder to find the necessary equipment for cutting on Steenbeck, be it tapes for the numbering machine, be it the viewing theatres for a double head viewing, that kind of a thing. The other thing is of course when push came to shove it was around about £150 grand cheaper to do it this way.

**What were the advantages of editing this way?**
Physically it was much easier because I didn't have to drag heavy cans of film off the rack and lace them up on the Steenbeck, all the time, all day for ten weeks. It's not the hardest thing in the world but I'm not getting any younger and they're quite heavy. It's also much easier and it's very quick on the Avid. Ken would say 'Can we look at take three?' and he'd be about to do a text or

make a phone call because he'd got used to having a bit of time using film – I'd have to take one roll off, go and get the cans, lace up another roll, wind it down to take three... this way it's click, click and it's there.

**Were there any disadvantages to cutting on computer?**
Nothing devastating although frankly now I'm sat in the cutting room on my own so there isn't the camaraderie if you like and the teamwork that you used to get with film editing. But it is more than compensated for in many ways by the fact that now George Fenton has done some rough versions of the music that we're probably going to use and they're in the computer and added onto the cutting copy. To do that would have been quite expensive on film. I can do fade outs and fade ins. I put a rough version of the titles on the film in a matter of, you know, minutes. I could adjust levels of sound, we could do a little rough grade of the colour on the picture. There were so many things that we could do and I know that Ken, sort of, appreciated it.

**You've worked on many of Ken Loach's films. How does _I, Daniel Blake_ fit in to the catalogue?**
It's a small Ken Loach film. None of our films are that big but _Land and Freedom_, _The Wind That Shakes the Barley_ and _Carla's Song_ were big war films, and compared to them this is on the small side – but we've had such good viewings that we're very encouraged by it to be honest. It's a very intimate, simple piece really. There's lots of politics but none of it is in any way obvious – it's not a polemic I don't think – which is really good. And there are little funny things going on throughout – a dog having a crap, a parcel being delivered – which I think really work well. That's down to Ken's expertise and the actors of course of making it all work so well.

# Film Credits

Sixteen Films
Why Not Productions
Wild Bunch
BFI
BBC Films
Les Films du Fleuve
France 2 Cinéma
Canal +
France Télévisions
Le Pacte
Cinéart
Ciné +
VOO and Be tv

| | |
|---|---|
| Director | Ken Loach |
| Producer | Rebecca O'Brien |
| Screenplay | Paul Laverty |
| Executive Producers | Pascal Caucheteux |
| | Grégoire Sorlat |
| | Vincent Maraval |
| Production Designers | Fergus Clegg |
| | Linda Wilson |
| Photography | Robbie Ryan |
| Recordist | Ray Beckett |
| Sound Editor | Kevin Brazier |
| Casting | Kahleen Crawford |
| Costume Designer | Joanne Slater |
| Assistant Director | David Gilchrist |
| Line Producer | Eimhear McMahon |
| Editor | Jonathan Morris |
| Music | George Fenton |

| | |
|---|---|
| Dan | Dave Johns |
| Katie | Hayley Squires |
| Daisy | Briana Shann |
| Dylan | Dylan Phillip McKiernan |
| Ann | Kate Rutter |
| Sheila | Sharon Percy |
| China | Kema Sikazwe |
| Piper | Steven Richens |
| | |
| Assessor | Amanda Payne |
| At the Sawmill | Chris McGlade |
| | Shaun Prendergast |
| | Gavin Webster |
| Specialist Nurse | Sammy T. Dobson |
| Neighbour With Dog | Mickey Hutton |
| Postman | Colin Coombs |
| Benefit Enquiry Line Advisor | David Murray |
| Floor Manager | Stephen Clegg |
| Jobcentre Guard | Andy Kidd |
| Stan Li | Dan Li |
| Librarian | Jane Birch |
| Students | Kimberley Blair Smith |
| | Junior Atilassi |
| C.V. Instructor | John Sumner |
| Harry Edwards | Dave Turner |
| Foodbank | Kathleen Germain |
| | Jackie Robinson |
| | Christine Wood |
| Supermarket Guard Ivan | Micky McGregor |
| Supermarket Manager | Neil Stuart Morton |
| Decision Maker | Roy McCartney |
| Furniture Dealer | Steve Halliday |
| Business Woman | Julie Nicholson |
| Woman in house | Viktoria Kay |
| Scotsman | Malcolm Shields |
| Police | Bryn Jones |
| | Helen Dixon |
| Senior Police Officer | Gary Jacques |
| Welfare Rights Officer | Mick Laffey |

and
Patricia Roberts, Yvonne Maher, Susan Robinson, Mike Milligan,
Laura Jane Barnes-Martin, Harriet Ghost, Brian Scurr

| | |
|---|---|
| Production Co-ordinator | Courtney Jones |
| Assistant Production Co-ordinators | Lucy Marr |
| | Chris Bevan |
| Production Runners | Patrick Jones, |
| | Emily Tillman |
| Producer's Assistant | Niamh Hayes |
| Director's Assistant | Ann Cattrall |
| 2nd Assistant Director | Jamie Hamer |
| 3rd Assistant Director | Henry Gordon |
| Floor Runner | La'Toyah McDonald |
| Script Supervisor | Heather Storr |
| Stills Photographer | Joss Barratt |
| Titles Design | Martin Butterworth |
| | Creative Partnership |
| Casting Associate | Caroline Stewart |
| Casting Assistant | Polly Malloch |
| Focus Puller | Andrew O'Reilly |
| Clapper Loaders | Joachim Philippe |
| | Léo Lefèvre |
| Camera Trainee | Ellen Pickering |
| Steadicam Operator/B-Cam | Matt Fisher |
| Location Manager | Mark Gales |
| Unit Manager | Dave Gales |
| Location Assistants | Aaron Blackburn |
| | James Goodwin |
| Boom Operator | Neal Skillen |
| Sound Trainee | Alex Lewis |
| Additional Boom Operator | Michael Duddy |
| Gaffer | Simon Magee |
| Best Boy | Dries Houben |
| Generator Operator | François Tiberghien |
| Additional Electricians | Pete Murphy |
| | Ross O'Brien |
| Standby Art Director | Caroline Barton |
| Prop Buyer | Amy Cooper Goodrich |

| | |
|---|---|
| Petty Cash Buyer | Zoe Robinson |
| Art Department Assistant | Benjamin Davis |
| Prop Master | Tom Pleydell Pearce |
| Dressing Props | Don Santos |
| | John Condron |
| Standby Props | Dominic Byles |
| Construction Manager | Colin Dent |
| Painter | Craig Orton |
| | |
| Make-up and Hair Designer | Anita Brolly |
| Make-up Trainee | Kim Brown |
| Make-up Daily | Danielle Jones |
| | |
| Wardrobe Supervisor | Vivienne Race |
| Costume Assistant | Nisha Williams |
| | |
| Production Accountant | Isabel Chick |
| Accountant | Habib Rahman |
| | |
| Fine Food Catering | Susan Humphreys |
| | Gareth Harding |
| | Ellie Goff |
| Transport | Brian Robson |
| | Ron Robson |
| Rushes Runner | Steven Armstrong |
| | |
| Computer Graphics by Red Frog | David Loveridge |
| | Adeel Punnu |
| | |
| Assistant Editors | Alison Carter-Goulden |
| | Erline O'Donovan |
| | |
| Effects Editor/Foley Recordist | Robert Brazier |
| Dialogue/Foley Editor | Ben Brazier |
| Foley Artist | Rowena Wilkinson |
| | Sue Harding |
| | |
| Post Production | Molinare |
| Colourist | Gareth Spensley |
| Online Editor | Nick Anderson |
| Facility Post Production Manager | Louise Stewart |
| Offline Editing Equipment | Salon Editing Equipment |

| | |
|---|---|
| Camera and Lighting Equipment | Eye Lite |
| Film Stock | Kodak Belgium |
| Laboratory Services | iDailies |
| Neg Cutter | Steve Farman, PNC |
| Post Production Script | Sapex Scripts |
| | |
| Insurance | Media Insurance Brokers |
| Script Clearances | Debbie Banbury-Morley |
| | |
| Re-recording Mixers | Andrew Caller |
| | Adam Scrivener |
| Sound Mix Technicians | John Skehill |
| | Michael Clayton |
| Re-recording | Pinewood Studios |

Music recorded and mixed by Mat Bartram at Angel Studios

| | |
|---|---|
| Pro Tools Recordist | Chris Parker |
| Music Preparation | Samuel Pegg |
| Score Musicians | Cello: Caroline Dale |
| | Violin: Jess Murphy |

'Sailing By' (Ronald Binge)
Published by Mozart Edition (Great Britain) Ltd
Performed by The Perry/Gardner Orchestra
Conducted by Ronald Binge
Licensed courtesy of Mozart Edition (Great Britain) Ltd

THANK YOU
John James McArdle, Black Triangle Campaign; Maryhill Foodbank;
Julie Webster; Mike Vallance, The Autonomous Centre of Edinburgh
and Edinburgh Coalition Against Poverty; Dr. Stephen Carty; Dr.
Margaret Craig; Prof. David Webster; Inclusion Scotland; Bill Scott;
Jeanette Campbell; Chris Orr; Dundee Unemployed Workers Network;
Tony Cox; Willie Denholme; Vince Logan;  Nuneaton: Doorway,
Carol Gallagher; Jack Pickering; Dave Ginnelly; Stoke-on-Trent: Susan
Bruce; Nottingham: Lisa McKenzie; St Anns Advice Centre; POW
Advice; Kenny MacAskill; Ruth Smith; Emma Bell; Kevin Garvey;

A very special thanks to workers within the DWP and PCS Union
who provided us with invaluable information but who must remain
anonymous.

Alasdair Hill, NUFC; Bob Whelans, Newcastle Labour Club; Rev.
Allan Dickinson, Bay Foodbank; Gillian Hewitson, Newcastle Futures;
Gillian Atkinson, Tomorrow's People; Claire Webster Saaremets,
Skimstone Arts; Neil Baird & Val Lynch, Changing Lives; Phil Old -
Armed Forces & Veterans Launchpad; Fran Heathcote; Judy Cowgill,
Hawthorn Primary School; Helen Coker – Peanuts Casting; Maxine
Brown & Space 2; Kerry & Helen – Walker YMCA; Christian Seradura
and Fabien Snoeck; Nicolas Livecchi; Laurent Berthou; Warren Thomas
and staff at Hoochie Coochie; the County Hotel and Hampton by
Hilton; staff and volunteers at Broadacre House;
and Shea, the three legged dog.

| | |
|---|---|
| Welfare Rights Advisor | Ruth Smith |
| Lawyers | Stephen Grosz |
| | Tamsin Allen |
| | Bindmans LLP |
| For Why Not Productions | Rosa Attab |
| | Benjamin Toussaint, |
| | Pauline Bénard |
| For Wild Bunch | Carole Baraton |
| | Emmanuelle Castro |
| For Les Films du Fleuve | Delphine Tomson |
| | Tania Antonioli |
| For BFI | Ben Roberts |
| | Fiona Morham |
| | Will Evans |
| | Clare Coulter |
| | Sofia Neves |
| | Emma Kayee |
| For BBC Films | Christine Langan |
| | Joe Oppenheimer |
| | Michael Wood |
| | Zoe Brown |
| | Livy Sandler |
| | Jacqui Barr |
| | Ruth Sanders |

Produced with the support of:
Brahim Chioua, Valérie Boyer, Bertrand Hassini-Bonnette, Didier
Lupfer, Laurent Hassid, Kristina Zimmermann, Anne Flamant, Jean
Labadie, Philippe Logie, VOO et Be tv; The Tax Shelter of the Belgian
Federal Government; Isabelle Molhant, Casa Kafka Pictures; Belfius

Collection Agent      Freeway CAM B.V
International Sales     Wild Bunch S.A

A British / French / Belgian Co-Production under the
European Convention on Cinematographic Co-Production

Filmed on location in Newcastle Upon Tyne.

Made with the support of the BFI's Film Fund
© Sixteen Tyne Limited, Why Not Productions, Wild Bunch,
Les Films du Fleuve,
British Broadcasting Corporation, France 2 Cinéma
and The British Film Institute 2016